HINTS

✦ F O R   T H E ✦

HIGHLY EFFECTIVE INSTRUCTOR

SURVIVAL SKILLS FOR THE TECHNICAL TRAINER

FIFTH EDITION

AMERICAN TECHNICAL PUBLISHERS
Orland Park, Illinois

W. R. Miller
M. F. Miller

American Technical Publishers, Inc., Editorial Staff

Editor in Chief:
    Jonathan F. Gosse
Vice President—Editorial:
    Peter A. Zurlis
Assistant Production Manager:
    Nicole D. Bigos
Technical Editor:
    Cathy A. Scruggs
Copy Editor:
    Catherine A. Mini
Cover Design:
    Richard O. Davis
Illustration/Layout:
    Alex C. Tulik

5 6 7 8 9 – 17 – 9 8 7 6 5 4 3 2 1

Printed in the United States of America

ISBN 978-0-8269-4148-0

 This book is printed on recycled paper.

CONTENTS

HINTS FOR THE HIGHLY EFFECTIVE INSTRUCTOR

ABOUT THE AUTHORS

Dr. Wilbur R. Miller has taught at both the secondary and postsecondary levels and served as dean of the College of Education at the University of Missouri-Columbia. He has received numerous awards and citations, including the Distinguished Service Award from the National Center for Research in Career and Technical Education and the University of Missouri Alumni Faculty Award.

Dr. Miller has authored or co-authored eight books and many periodicals, monographs, and bulletins. He serves as a consultant to schools and industry in the U.S. and other countries. Dr. Miller has served as Associate Vice-President and Vice-President for Development at Auburn University.

Dr. Marie F. Miller received a PhD in technical education from the University of Missouri-Columbia. She has received many awards and citations for her professional contributions, including the Distinguished Alumni Award from the University of Wisconsin-Stout and the Undergraduate Teaching Excellence Award from the Auburn University Alumni Association.

Dr. Miller has authored and co-authored six books and has written numerous articles and papers. She serves on the Board of Editors for the *Online Journal of Workforce Education* and *Scientific Journals International* (SJI). In addition, she serves as Test Center Coordinator for Alabama for the National Occupational Competency Testing Institute. Dr. Miller also holds the Endowed Mildred Cheshire Fraley Distinguished Professorship in the Department of Educational Foundations, Leadership, and Technology at Auburn University.

INTRODUCTION

HINTS FOR THE HIGHLY EFFECTIVE INSTRUCTOR

An instructional program is most effective when the instructor understands and addresses the complexities of the teaching-learning process. *Hints for the Highly Effective Instructor: Survival Skills for the Technical Trainer* includes strategies and techniques for making teaching and learning effective. Designed for both new and experienced instructors, the information presented is organized for quick access and easy implementation. Instructional methods and resources, content curation, assessments, massive open online courses (MOOCs), and accommodation of special populations are included. Each chapter concludes with a self-assessment that can be used to evaluate instructional strategies and techniques.

This valuable, concise reference can be used as a guide for implementing new instructional programs or for affirming the attributes of existing successful instructional programs.

The Publisher

Instructor Characteristics

Hints for the Highly Effective Instructor

An instructor's personal characteristics come through in the classroom setting. Attitudes, values, and communication style all influence the way learners respond. An instructor's professional behavior can serve to model behavior expected in the field. Also, instructors are responsible for their own professional development, which can help them stay up-to-date and keep learners informed about current issues in industry.

Convey Enthusiasm for Teaching and Respect for Learners

Many variables contribute to an instructor's effectiveness. Personal attributes of instructors such as intelligence, knowledge of subject matter, and background are important in the teaching-learning process. Effective teaching involves a complex set of variables, making the measurement of teaching effectiveness by using standardized instruments difficult and often unreliable. Effective instructors are those who can bring about changed behavior in the learners.

Instructors who are excited about teaching and learning convey a positive and accepting attitude to learners. They communicate the value of attaining certain skills and knowledge and hold high expectations for themselves and their learners. Also, effective instructors show consideration for different personalities and learning styles and preferences. Individual differences bring strengths, not weaknesses, to the classroom. Instructors should treat participants in specialized training and workshops with respect. In fact, an instructor's acceptance of and concern for the learner is one of the most important factors in fostering an individual's motivation to learn.

Many learners have had unpleasant experiences in school. An instructor's professional appearance and courteous behavior toward learners and other school personnel communicate positive intentions and a willingness to help.

Practice Equitable and Fair Treatment

Learners, like instructors, have different personalities, expectations, interests, needs, and ability levels. Content should be presented so that individuals of all ability levels can understand. If an instructor shows favoritism and special consideration toward some learners, all learners are affected. Those who are favored may mislead instructors into thinking that they are doing a good job of teaching, while those who are not favored will quickly become discouraged.

From time to time, assignments may need to be varied. This is especially true when instruction is individualized; however, there should be adequate and challenging assignments and activities for everyone participating in a particular learning situation.

Practice Sound Judgment and Diplomacy

Instructors should not show anger or argue with learners during class; this demonstrates poor judgment on the part of the instructor. Occasionally, a learner may know or pretend to know more about a certain topic than the instructor. In such cases, the instructor should avoid a confrontation with the learner in the presence of other learners. The instructor has nothing to gain, but risks losing the respect of the class by insisting on being right. In such cases, instructors can avoid criticism by tactfully avoiding an open argument until the facts can be collected. Instructors should be diplomatic and know how to say, "I don't know, but I'll find out," or "Let's check that out."

Even when a learner disagrees with an instructor, it is very difficult to argue with diplomacy. In any case, whether the instructor is right or wrong, the documented facts should promptly be brought back to the class.

Cooperate with Colleagues and Practice Teamwork

Effective training programs operate in an efficient and businesslike manner. It is a mistake to fail to collaborate and cooperate with colleagues. Management can be effective only when there is teamwork. Cooperation is needed to conserve the time of the instructors, learners, and other personnel. Instructors who go above and beyond the minimal expectations of being a good team player are positive role models for their learners and garner the respect of their colleagues.

Instructors may be called upon or choose to team teach, dividing the instruction into areas of individual strengths or interests. For example, one instructor may conduct large group sessions and another may work with learners who are advanced or who may need additional instruction and support. Team teaching requires members of the team to make joint decisions about individual responsibilities, methods of instructional delivery, and the use of time, materials, and other resources.

BE PUNCTUAL

Instructors who are in the classroom or laboratory organizing their work before the scheduled time for class to start may find learners getting to class early or at least on schedule. Instructors who come to the class at precisely the scheduled time or a few minutes late may find that learners come in late. Learners may assume that if the instructor is not there on time, they do not need to be either.

The importance of a good example on the part of the instructor should be recognized. Being prompt shows initiative and helps develop the habit of getting to the job on time. In addition, being in the classroom before the scheduled time gives the instructor and the learners a few minutes to settle in and prepare. An added benefit is that the learners will have an opportunity to talk with the instructor and others in the class before formal instruction starts. This can be very important as learners may have questions about the class or laboratory assignment, other courses, or career opportunities.

MAINTAIN A PROFESSIONAL APPEARANCE

Participants in specialized training workshops and technical education programs often look to instructors for standards of behavior. An instructor may be one of only a few role models for these learners. Instructors who come to class clean and well-groomed project a positive image to the learners.

Appropriate dress may range from smart casual to work uniforms depending on the type of training and work to be done. Personal protective equipment may be an important and necessary part of dress. The manner in which an instructor dresses demonstrates to learners the standard for acceptable dress, and in turn, what is expected and accepted in the industry. Instructors who care about their own appearance model behavior that will stay with most learners throughout their careers.

MOTIVATE AND ENCOURAGE ALL LEARNERS

When instructors provide support and encouragement, people learn more. If instructors are not supportive and encouraging, the learners may learn less, develop indifferent attitudes, doubt their self-worth, become frustrated, or leave the instructional program. All learners deserve the opportunity to experience success. Checking and evaluating assignments and providing immediate feedback are excellent means of encouragement. Learners want instructors to comment on the completeness, accuracy, and overall quality of their work in both the classroom and the laboratory.

Instructors should encourage learners who have done their best, even if the overall quality of the work is not at the desired level. When a learner is not performing up to par, the instructor should comment on areas in which the learner does well, and not emphasize the learner's mistakes. Such phrases as, "No, that is wrong," or "That is not right," are far more discouraging than phrases such as, "Let's try that again," or "That is a good start, how can you improve on it?" Generally, people will put forth high levels of effort if they feel it will help them meet their goals and satisfy their needs.

When a learner makes a comment or offers an answer that is partly correct, the instructor should comment immediately on the part that is correct without criticizing or reprimanding the learner. Only through encouragement and reinforcement will most learners continue to improve. When a learner's work begins to improve, instructors should provide praise and recognize the improvement. However, complimenting a learner every time the learner makes a comment or answers a question correctly is not advisable. Excessive compliments may be embarrassing to the shy learner or may be misunderstood by the other learners as a show of favoritism. This is particularly true when the learner's contribution is rather ordinary. Each time a learner makes a comment or answers a question correctly, the instructor should acknowledge that the contribution is correct. This way all learners will know that the comment is correct.

USE EFFECTIVE COMMUNICATION SKILLS

The ability to communicate effectively is key to getting a job, keeping a job, and being promoted in a job. All occupations continue to require more sophistication, not only in the technology of the field, but also in the way in which individuals communicate. It is not surprising that national initiatives and mandates require the integration of technical education and academic subjects. For this reason, effective communication skills should be of vital concern to instructors. For example, instructors who use correct English and proper pronunciation and spelling are modeling to learners that there is more to preparing for a job in an industrial or technical field than simply possessing the required technical knowledge and skills.

Instructors should take care to speak slowly and clearly so that learners can understand the vocabulary, especially the technical terminology, needed in their area of interest. Instructors should go beyond the definition of a term, if necessary, to illustrate the use of technical terminology in the subject area. Effective communication, both written and oral, requires that definitions, instructions, illustrations, assignments, and other explanations be presented in technically correct language that is easily understood. An instructor should always review and check all handout materials and tests to ensure that they do not contain misspelled words, poor punctuation, or inconsistencies.

Technical and scientific fields of study use specialized terminology or nomenclature. Nomenclature gives special meaning to words when they are used within the context of the specific field of study. Many textbooks on technical subjects include a glossary covering the nomenclature for that subject. For example, "predictive maintenance" and "programmable controllers" are examples of nomenclature used for industrial maintenance; "solenoids" and "variable-frequency drives" are examples of nomenclature used for electrical motor controls; and "powers" and "roots" are nomenclature used in mathematics. Use of appropriate nomenclature by an instructor is vital to building a learner's knowledge base.

After learners complete an instructional program, they should be prepared to incorporate their new knowledge and skills into their work. Learners will be expected to interact with customers and clients, prepare and read work orders, work as members of a team, and participate in discussions related to workplace procedures.

PRACTICE PROFESSIONAL USE OF ELECTRONIC COMMUNICATIONS

Instructors use electronic communication, not only for instructional purposes, but also to interact with individual learners, other instructors, and industry representatives. Email and voice mail are as important as face-to-face conversations because they represent both the person and the organization. Consequently, special care should be taken to ensure that voice mail and email messages are clear, concise, accurate, courteous, and friendly. When the message is confidential or of a sensitive nature, email and voice mail may not be the best communication methods as neither ensures privacy.

A few general guidelines can be helpful to reinforce effective use of voice mail. It is important to speak slowly and clearly when leaving a voice mail message. Also, it is good practice to give your name, telephone number, and extension number before leaving your message and to repeat them when you are finished. A brief message specifying what the receiver should do—call you back, wait for your return call, etc., should be left. The date and time that you called and the best time for you to receive a return call should be indicated.

When a cell phone is used, courteous behavior should be observed. Cell phone users should keep cell phone conversations brief when in the company of others. Instructors and the learners should turn off cell phones during instruction.

Like voice mail messages, email messages should be brief. The frequency with which email is used for communication makes it prohibitive for busy people to read long messages. Email messages should open with the appropriate salutation, depending on the relationship the sender has with the recipient.

Messages should be typed using uppercase and lowercase letters as appropriate. Using all uppercase letters may be interpreted by the receiver as shouting. Correct spelling, grammar, and punctuation should be used. Messages should be reread and edited before they are sent. It is best to avoid using abbreviations such as BTW for "by the way," emoticons such as the smiley face, and humor. Closings such as "Sincerely Yours," or "Very Respectfully," or simply "Thanks" add a nice touch to an email. The email should end with the sender's name, title, telephone number, or other appropriate contact information.

Text messaging (texting) is the common term that refers to using a short message service. This technology provides instant communication and advantages but, like cell phone use, requires proper etiquette. In the classroom, texting should be avoided. Reading a text message during a conversation, like listening to a voice mail message, is rude behavior. Messages received can be answered at the appropriate time to avoid distracting the class. In addition, the ability to send text messages should be controlled in an examination setting to eliminate the possibility of cheating.

Text messages are documents that could be accessed by others and require the same care in tone and accuracy as email messages. Slang and inappropriate abbreviations should be avoided. Sensitive information is best communicated in private by a phone conversation.

The ability to communicate effectively carries over from the classroom and laboratory to securing support for the technical training program. Instructors need to work with their industry counterparts and other industry leaders to ensure an up-to-date and viable program. Technical education instructors who form and participate in special industry training advisory councils are better informed of the needs and interests of a particular organization. Instructors who are able to articulate the strengths and needs of their programs clearly and coherently will undoubtedly receive a higher level of support and commitment than those who cannot.

Practice Active Listening

Active listening is as important as speaking clearly. Research shows that most people use only about 25% to 30% of their listening potential. Most people are distracted constantly by either external or internal noise. Noises generated by machinery, equipment, or coworkers are good examples of external noise. Disinterest in a subject, dislike for the speaker, preoccupation with other responsibilities, or simply being too tired to listen are all examples of internal noise. Most people speak at a rate of 125 to 150 words per minute; most people can listen to approximately 400 to 500 words per minute.

Active listening takes dedication and training. Active listening is paramount for effective teaching. Instructors should practice the following guidelines to improve their active listening skills:

- Make and maintain direct eye contact with learners when they are speaking.
- Get involved in the learner's comments by asking questions or acknowledging their comments.
- Do not interrupt the speaker (unless absolutely necessary due to behavior such as improper comments or language).
- Do not change the subject or direct the speaker's comments or questions until you are sure that you understand the intent of the comment or question.
- Keep your emotions under control.
- Respond in a way that lets the speaker know that the speaker's comments or questions were communicated clearly and understood.
- Do not prejudge the learner.
- Empathize with learners who are trying, yet may be having a difficult time grasping the material.
- Ask relevant questions that show that you are listening, interested, and caring.
- Remember: Patience is a virtue!

KEEP ACCURATE RECORDS

Accurate record keeping is vital to the operation, maintenance, and credibility of a program. Requests from other instructors and supervisors for information, assistance, or a special report should not be delayed, unless the reason for the delay is appropriate and explained to those who are waiting for the information. Failure to observe requests for certain information may mean a loss of time and money. Records are necessary, and individual reports are needed in the compilation of final reports and records.

Just as instructors have a set of rules for their classrooms and laboratories, educational institutions have sets of rules that everyone is expected to follow. When a rule appears to be unsound, the instructor should mention the flawed rule to the supervisor along with suggested changes for improvement.

MODEL PROFESSIONAL DEVELOPMENT

Professional development in the areas of teaching and learning is just as important as knowledge in a subject area. Although this is one area often overlooked and sometimes discounted by instructors of technical subjects, developing and increasing professional competencies plays a major role in the teaching-learning process.

New legislation, state codes and policies, and program guidelines are presented at industry-supported conferences and seminars, as well as state-supported professional development activities.

Universities often offer special courses, seminars, and workshops to help update and upgrade the technical knowledge and professional competencies of instructors, as well as to facilitate the acquisition of new knowledge and competencies. Professional associations provide another source of information through special conferences, meetings, and materials to enhance the professional development of instructors.

SUMMARY

Personal characteristics play an important role in the teaching-learning process. Respect for the learners and their needs, interests, and abilities and enthusiasm for the subject matter are paramount to creating a positive learning environment. Encouragement through providing opportunities for growth and development helps to create situations and conditions in which learners will be self-motivated. It is up to the instructor to provide guidance, direction, and reassurance to learners. All individuals deserve to be treated fairly and equitably. Favoritism creates situations that are counterproductive to learning.

Promptness and attentiveness in the classroom communicate a professional attitude to learners specifically and toward education generally. Successful instructors serve as role models for learners, not only through their actions, but also through their appearance.

Effective communication skills are necessary for success both in and out of the classroom and laboratory. Participants in specialized training programs and workshops need to communicate effectively in person and when using any form of electronic communication. Active listening skills are imperative for effective teaching.

Teamwork helps ensure successful and productive training programs. Instructors may be responsible for completing administrative tasks in a timely manner to ensure support for educational programs.

Instructors who stay current in their field of expertise usually earn the respect and admiration of their colleagues, managers, and learners. It is not enough to stay current only in industrial or technical subject areas. Those who want to serve others through the profession of teaching should also participate in special courses, workshops, and conferences to develop and enhance their use of instructional technology and their planning, teaching, monitoring, and evaluation skills.

Self-Assessment Checklist

HINTS FOR THE HIGHLY EFFECTIVE INSTRUCTOR

INSTRUCTOR CHARACTERISTICS

Yes	No	Needs Attention	
☐	☐	☐	1. Do you look forward to going to work each day?
☐	☐	☐	2. Could a visitor tell you are the instructor by your attire?
☐	☐	☐	3. Does your attire reflect that expected in industry?
☐	☐	☐	4. Do you arrive early to the classroom or laboratory?
☐	☐	☐	5. Do you encourage learners to come to class on time or even earlier?
☐	☐	☐	6. Do you encourage learners to talk with one another and with you before the class is scheduled to start?
☐	☐	☐	7. Are you interested in learners' progress and growth?
☐	☐	☐	8. Are you an active listener?
☐	☐	☐	9. Are you comfortable talking to other instructors?
☐	☐	☐	10. Are you comfortable talking to administrators?
☐	☐	☐	11. Are you willing to admit your mistakes?
☐	☐	☐	12. Do you handle differences in opinion diplomatically?
☐	☐	☐	13. Do you look for opportunities to praise learners?
☐	☐	☐	14. Do you demonstrate the proper etiquette for email communication, phone use, and text messaging?
☐	☐	☐	15. Are you able to settle differences of opinion and address disciplinary problems without engaging in confrontations with learners?
☐	☐	☐	16. Do you have a cooperative attitude toward your colleagues?
☐	☐	☐	17. Do you offer ideas to the administration to improve your program?
☐	☐	☐	18. Do you interact with leaders in your field?
☐	☐	☐	19. Do you volunteer for additional responsibilities?
☐	☐	☐	20. Do you stay current in your field by taking courses and/or attending seminars and conferences?

PREPARATION FOR INSTRUCTION

2

HINTS FOR THE HIGHLY EFFECTIVE INSTRUCTOR

Effective training programs do not just happen; they are the product of careful planning and preparation. The instructional session, whether conducted as a class, a workshop, or a seminar, requires planning. In all instructional settings, lesson plans or agendas must be created, objectives must be stated, and equipment and facilities must be made ready for use. Also, all the materials should be prepared and software loaded ahead of time. For a workshop or seminar held in an industrial setting, it will be necessary to conduct a needs assessment, and the program will need to be publicized.

DEVELOP A LESSON PLAN OR AGENDA

In a classroom setting, the instructor works from a lesson plan, also known as an instructional plan. (Lesson plan development will be addressed in Chapter 3— Instructional Planning.) In a workshop or seminar setting, the instructor works from an agenda. The purpose of both is to help the instructor stay on track and stay focused. An agenda should be prepared several weeks prior to the workshop or seminar. **See Figure 2-1.**

WRITE OBJECTIVES FOR EACH INSTRUCTIONAL SESSION

Clearly stated objectives provide direction and guidance for the instructional session. Written objectives are a necessary tool in any type of instructional setting and should be written early to allow the instructor enough time to prepare the necessary materials. In addition, clearly stated objectives provide a framework for the learners and for evaluating the results of the instruction. Each objective should include specific conditions, tools, or materials required to achieve the objective. In an industrial setting, objectives should be written after the needs assessment results are analyzed.

SAMPLE AGENDA

Workshop Agenda–Americans with Disabilities Act
Industrial Site 1–Training Room B

Instructor Facilitator: Chris Johnson
Special Guests: Marty Green, State Representative
Bill Fare, Attorney-at-Law

Welcome and Introductions

Overview of Workshop

Overview of Societal Contexts for Individuals with Disabilities

ADA Definitions

Overview of Legal Requirements
• Employer requirements for compliance
• Special situations and specific exclusions
• Nondiscriminatory qualification standards and selection criteria
• Nondiscrimination in the hiring process (recruitment, applications, pre-employment inquiries, and testing)

Health and Safety
• Direct threats to health and safety of self or others
• Direct threat to food handling

Confidentiality
• Post/offer examinations or inquiries
• Limitations on use of medical information

Implications for Scotchdale Manufacturing

Wrap-up–Questions and Comments

Workshop Evaluation

Adjourn

Figure 2-1. In a workshop or seminar setting, the instructor uses an agenda to guide the session.

PREPARE INSTRUCTIONAL MATERIALS

It is the instructor's responsibility to prepare instructional materials. Each instructional session will have its own unique characteristics and goals. The critical question for the instructor is, "How much skill and/or knowledge do I expect learners to have and by what date?" Often, the instructor can purchase commercial materials for the session.

A minimum of two or three weeks should be allotted to locate and/or prepare instructional materials. In an industrial setting, vendors may supply the training materials. In all cases, it is a good idea for instructors to develop an instructional materials resource file that lists contact information for various sources of instructional materials.

PowerPoint® is a presentation software program commonly used in instructional settings. It includes templates for formatting slides, sample graphics such as charts and figures, an assortment of background colors and designs, and several slide presentation options. PowerPoint presentations can be modified to reflect specific instructional needs. Videos and animations can be embedded in slides and accessed for enhanced instruction. Although there are many options available for format, color, and graphics, each presentation must be effective for learners. The following general guidelines should be used to create PowerPoint presentations:

- Use a font size large enough to allow learners to easily read the slide from any location in the learning environment.
- Limit slide content to succinct points with sufficient space on each slide to prevent visual clutter.
- Use a format that enhances the flow of the information and delineates the main headings and subheadings.
- Use background colors and designs that contrast with the font color so that the text is easy to read.
- Use graphics and artwork that focus on instructional relevance.

It is also a good idea to prepare instructional materials that allow for flexibility in both use and time allocation to meet a variety of current and future needs. The materials should be sequenced in a logical order, with natural breaking points to allow for learner participation. In all cases, instructional materials should be double-checked for accuracy, completeness, and appearance. These materials should also contain correct content, grammar, and spelling. Instructional materials that are neat, clear, and attractive not only make a favorable impression, they also help to stimulate and motivate learning. Such materials speak well of the instructor and communicate to the learners the importance and value of the instruction.

SCHEDULE EQUIPMENT AND FACILITIES

Some instructors are fortunate enough to have equipment and facilities dedicated specifically to their program needs. However, in an organization where equipment and facilities are shared among several departments or units, it is critical that the equipment and facilities as well as any special tools be reserved ahead of time. A two-week notice is usually adequate; however, in some circumstances, such as a particularly busy time of the year, requests for equipment and facilities may need to be made more than two weeks in advance.

All equipment should be checked to ensure it is in safe working condition well before the session begins. Personal protective equipment, such as special clothing, shields, goggles, and gloves, should be available and in good condition. Facilities should be checked to ensure that there are adequate tables and chairs or workstations, that there is enough space for equipment such as projectors or screens, and that the learning environment is clean and comfortable.

Conduct a Needs Assessment

Prior to establishing a new course or instructional program, a needs assessment should be conducted. It is not unusual to conduct a needs assessment six months or more before instruction. This is particularly true when new products, equipment, processes, or policies are to be introduced. Some learners may not need training on specific kinds of equipment, others may need minimal training, and others may need extensive training. The type of training needs and the extent of the training should be determined before any actual planning is undertaken.

When feasible, it is a good idea for the instructor to organize an advisory committee (three to five members) to assist in the clarification and verification of training needs. Management and supervisory personnel as well as hourly workers are appropriate members on such a committee.

Senior workers often have accurate knowledge of the skills and knowledge that individuals need to have to perform their jobs effectively. Likewise, management and supervisory personnel may be aware of the type of training that individuals need. It is not uncommon for industrial trainers to be required to document the type of training needed and to provide a rationale for such training. The following steps may be used to conduct a needs assessment:

1. Select the population to be surveyed. Will information be collected for all employees in an organization, a sample of all employees, or a specific group of employees?
2. Include information on the interests, abilities, and career goals of the target population, as well as their training needs.
3. Set a timetable for completing the survey.
4. Develop the survey instrument using a standardized set of questions. **See Figure 2-2.** Printed or digital surveys, personal or telephone interviews, or ideas contributed through a company suggestion box are all acceptable methods for collecting needs assessment information.

5. Provide a brief explanation of the survey to the target population. This may be in the form of a cover letter or email, or it may suffice to include a statement or two at the top of the survey form. Depending on the information sought, provisions must be in place for submission of survey forms anonymously.

6. Conduct the survey. It may be necessary to follow up with some members of the target population who do not respond in a timely manner. A follow up may include an email message or a phone call to prospective participants reminding them to return the survey.

7. Document the information in a usable format.

SAMPLE NEEDS ASSESSMENT SURVEY

Employee Interest Survey—Employing Individuals with Disabilities

Directions: Read each item below and indicate the extent to which you would like to develop knowledge or skills about the item. Base your responses on what you believe would be most beneficial to your current job. Circle the number that corresponds to your response using the response categories provided.

1 = N = No need to know

2 = S = Slight importance—would like to know basic information

3 = I = Important—need to acquire knowledge/skills in this area

4 = E = Essential—highest area of need (use no more than two to three times.)

KNOWLEDGE/SKILL AREA	Extent of Need			
	N	S	I	E
1. Employment practices regulated by the ADA	1	2	3	4
2. Undue hardship limitations and employers	1	2	3	4
3. Types of reasonable accommodations	1	2	3	4
4. Actions that constitute discrimination	1	2	3	4
5. Health and safety issues and practices	1	2	3	4

Name: (optional)_____

Figure 2-2. A survey instrument is used as part of a needs assessment.

Analyze Needs Assessment Results

The instructor should have a plan for coding, recording, and analyzing the information after it is collected. A plan for recording and analyzing needs assessment information does not have to be complex. For example, using a blank survey form as a coding sheet, the instructor can tally the number of responses for each item. This method provides a sound basis for determining the number of individuals who need or are interested in a particular workshop or seminar.

Select Participants

After the needs assessment is completed and the results are analyzed, individuals who can benefit from the instruction should be invited to participate in the workshop or seminar. These individuals may express their interest directly or their supervisor may contact the training department. An accurate match between participants' level of ability and interests with workshop objectives is essential for effective and efficient instruction. In some instances, certain select groups must be included in a particular training session, such as when new equipment and procedures are introduced. Likewise, there may be instances when all employees should participate in an instructional workshop or seminar.

Publicize the Instructional Program

In an industrial setting, the instructional program needs to be publicized four to five weeks before it is scheduled to begin. Publicity can take on many forms. For example, announcements may be included in employees' mailboxes or special notices posted online and/or in visible locations throughout the facility.

Summary

In all instructional settings, a lesson plan or agenda should be prepared to allow learners an opportunity to preview the instructional program, workshop, or seminar. Clearly stated instructional objectives should communicate to learners what they will learn or should be able to do upon completion of the instructional program.

Instructional materials may be developed by the instructor or they may be obtained from commercial vendors. Accommodations for equipment and facilities should be prearranged with ample time to permit any required operating or safety checks and ensuing repairs. In addition, a plan should be developed to provide appropriate personal protective equipment, as well as for the storage and handling of hazardous materials.

Depending on the instructional program, workshop, or seminar, a needs assessment may need to be conducted. The needs assessment should help clarify the type of training needed and the extent of the training, and should identify potential participants. An advisory committee may be formed to help clarify educational needs. Participants should be selected on the basis of their needs, interests, and abilities.

Timing is important in advertising a workshop or seminar. Notices that are issued too far in advance are just as problematic as those issued too close to the workshop date. Time allotted for advertising will vary with the specific type of workshop offered, the needs of participants, and organizational policies.

Self-Assessment Checklist

HINTS FOR THE HIGHLY EFFECTIVE INSTRUCTOR

PREPARATION FOR INSTRUCTION

Yes	No	Needs Attention	
☐	☐	☐	1. Do you prepare instructional materials ahead of class time?
☐	☐	☐	2. Do you use a lesson (instructional) plan or agenda?
☐	☐	☐	3. Do you write clear objectives for each instructional session?
☐	☐	☐	4. Do you prepare instructional materials so that they can be used again in the future?
☐	☐	☐	5. Do you ensure that all instructional materials are clear and contain correct grammar, spelling, and punctuation?
☐	☐	☐	6. Do you make sure to schedule all the equipment that will be needed in advance?
☐	☐	☐	7. Do you ensure that the equipment being used is in safe and proper operating condition?
☐	☐	☐	8. Do you check the facility ahead of time to ensure that it will meet the needs of the session?
☐	☐	☐	9. Do you conduct needs assessments when necessary?
☐	☐	☐	10. Do you have a method for analyzing the results of any needs assessment that is conducted?
☐	☐	☐	11. Do you invite participants on the basis of their training needs, interests, and abilities?
☐	☐	☐	12. Do you publicize the instructional program?

INSTRUCTIONAL PLANNING

HINTS FOR THE HIGHLY EFFECTIVE INSTRUCTOR

One of the most important tasks of the instructor is to plan for instruction. A pre-assessment helps the instructor understand why a learner is in a particular instructional setting and what the learner's expectation is, as well as the learner's ability level. An instructor may need to rewrite materials, organize materials into manageable topics, or develop instructional aids to ensure that all learners benefit from instruction. A post-assessment lets the instructor and learners know whether the instructional objectives were achieved.

GATHER LEARNER INFORMATION

No two learners are the same. Before meaningful instruction can be planned, the instructor should gather information about the learners. There are several effective and efficient ways in which an instructor can do this. The instructor can engage in discussions with learners or ask them to complete an instructor-developed information form. Questions such as the following help to reveal the learners' interests, needs, and expectations:

- What are your best and worst subjects?
- What are your immediate career plans?
- How would you rate your computer skills?
- Have you ever taken an online course?
- How do you learn best?
- What type of work experience have you had?
- How do you spend your spare time?
- Is there any other information that would help facilitate your learning?

Instructor observations of learners are also an effective means of learning about their needs, interests, and abilities. For example, how do learners spend their free time in the classroom and laboratory? On what types of projects do they prefer to work? Do they prefer to work in a small group or alone? Are they proficient in communicating online? Answers to questions such as these indicate learner needs and interests.

Address Digital Natives and Digital Immigrants

An instructor can face many instructional challenges resulting from learner differences between digital natives (those who have grown up with digital technology) and digital immigrants (those who have adopted the use of digital technology later in life). Digital natives commonly view interaction with a computer as a natural activity. This allows them to more easily navigate to a solution when confronted with error messages, software problems, or hardware problems.

In contrast, digital immigrants typically lack computer knowledge and confidence. Without a basic comfort level, this makes learning to use and apply software more complicated. This also leads to learner frustration and distraction from the learning process. In these situations, the instructor is forced to divert attention from the class to learners lacking basic skills. Minimizing this interruption to the instructional experience is critical for overall success. As technology continues to be embedded in daily work and personal activities, the number of digital immigrants will decrease.

Strategies that can be used to address the divide between digital natives and digital immigrants include providing prerequisite classes that ensure baseline computer knowledge and skills, in-class instructional assistants, and software tutorials. Assessment of the computer skills required for the class and the anticipated computer skills of the learners prior to instruction will help with instructional planning, especially when teaching classes using sophisticated software.

Develop Learner-Centered Performance Objectives

An instructor's job is to assist learners in developing the knowledge, skills, and attitudes necessary to become productive workers and responsible citizens. Textbooks, instructional manuals, curriculum guides, and course outlines typically state the competencies that learners should be able to acquire and demonstrate upon completion of an instructional program. It is important for the instructor to clearly communicate to learners what knowledge, skills, and attitudes are needed to become successful.

Learner-centered performance objectives are the foundation of instructional planning. Performance objectives should include the following:

- an action word or phrase that describes what to do, such as "replace and adjust brake shoes"
- a statement of the condition under which the activity should be performed, such as "given a vehicle with worn brake shoes, a technical manual, and proper equipment and facilities"
- criteria for measuring whether the learner performed the activity successfully, such as "so that brakes function properly"

The time spent writing learner-centered objectives is time well spent. This type of planning facilitates learning and guides the entire instructional process.

Plan Ahead

Planning a lesson well in advance of the first class gives the instructor time to ensure that the different parts of the lesson are presented in the best sequence and all necessary aids are ready for use. Instructors who spend time getting organized for instruction after the class has begun will find that learners are tardy, inattentive, and not very motivated to learn. Instructors who are hasty may also find that they have failed to include safety instructions, learner exercises, or necessary visual aids.

A good instructor prepares for instruction by making the necessary copies, accessing video clips and Internet sites, staging handouts, and checking equipment in advance. References can be bookmarked for quick access to information required. All equipment and instructional resources should be located in the instructional room for maximum efficiency. General tasks for instructional preparation are common to all instructional units. **See Figure 3-1.**

Instructional Preparation Checklist

ORDER FOR DELIVERY BEFORE INSTRUCTION
- ☐ Textbooks, special learner kits, or activity packages
- ☐ Personal protective equipment
- ☐ Special software

ONE WEEK BEFORE INSTRUCTION
- ☐ Review lesson plan(s)
- ☐ Review appropriate textbook chapters, special learner kits, or activity packages
- ☐ Gather/prepare instructor-provided resources
- ☐ Review supplementary reference materials
- ☐ Review PowerPoint® slides or instructional media
- ☐ Review handouts, worksheets, activity sheets, and answer keys
- ☐ Duplicate copies of handouts, worksheets, and activity sheets
- ☐ Review and duplicate copies of pre- and post-assessments
- ☐ Reserve/obtain multimedia equipment

DAY OF INSTRUCTION
- ☐ Check condition of instructional facility
- ☐ Test multimedia equipment for proper operation
- ☐ Cue instructional media as required

Figure 3-1. A preparation checklist can help instructors prepare more efficiently.

Most instructors feel a little anxious before the start of a new course or seminar Being overprepared rather than underprepared helps an instructor overcome anxiety. Planning for icebreakers, such as asking learners to introduce themselves or each other, helps learners feel at ease. Likewise, the instructor should not hesitate to share some personal background or special interests with the learners. Such openness lets learners know that the instructor is willing to share information.

Another anxiety-reducing technique is to have a small group activity planned for the first meeting. This not only helps individuals become acquainted with one another, it is an excellent method for setting the tone for the course or seminar.

Develop a Course of Study or Instructional Outline

A course of study or instructional outline presents an overview of the entire course and may be thought of as a teaching plan for the course. A course of study or instructional outline lists the major subject-matter topics and the sequence of the material to be presented. This allows the instructor to plan the proper pace by which specific course objectives can be fulfilled.

When developing the course of study or instructional outline, consideration should be given to the course objectives, the length of the course, and the instructional facilities available. Material should be presented from the simple to the complex, and new information should build on previous information and provide transfer of similar principles and concepts to different applications. Important components of a course of study or instructional outline include the following:

- name of the course
- course objectives
- list of the major units to be presented
- informational topics (discussion, lecture, readings, etc.)
- safety considerations
- equipment needed
- demonstrations
- instructional methods
- supplementary aids
- learning activities
- formative assessment activities
- summative assessments

DEVELOP A LESSON PLAN

A well-planned lesson, including the acquisition of appropriate teaching aids, equipment, and learning materials, makes the job of teaching much easier for the instructor and of greater value to learners. A lesson plan should be developed and followed for each classroom or laboratory session. The lesson plan should include the following important teaching information:

- the purpose of the lesson
- learner objectives
- a brief activity or exercise to focus learner attention on the content to be presented
- key elements of content such as specialized terminology, information, concepts, and procedures
- plans for demonstrations of how the information, concepts, or procedures can be applied
- learner activities that encourage visual, auditory, and kinesthetic learning
- planned opportunities for instructor-led and instructor-guided practice
- planned questions to check for learner understanding
- independent learner exercises
- resources needed to teach the lesson
- planned conclusion to the lesson
- a method of assessment and follow-up

Lesson planning is easier when instructors follow a specified format. A predetermined format helps an instructor organize a presentation and assures that all necessary areas of planning have been addressed. In addition, the instructor can know at a glance where to find information each time a lesson is taught. A lesson plan based on the four-step method of teaching—preparation, presentation, application, and evaluation is very effective. **See Figure 3-2.**

Using the same format for each lesson and numbering each section allows the instructor to view each component at a glance, thereby easing the transition from one phase of instruction to the next. The lesson plan may vary depending upon instructor preference, the content to be presented, and the objectives to be achieved. Related Internet resources, journal articles, manufacturer technical bulletins, and instructor-created worksheets can be added so that they are readily available. Notes, instructional cues, and questions are added as needed by the instructor.

FOUR-STEP LESSON PLAN FORMAT	
LESSON PLAN #86	
PREPARATION	Notes (Safety; Strategies; What Worked, etc.)
Classroom Preparation – *List everything you need to do and every item you need to implement the lesson (e.g., time, setting, materials, equipment, etc.).* **Preparatory Assignments** – *List any prior work or preparation learners need to complete in order to be ready for the lesson.* **Introduction/Motivation** – *List an activity that will motivate learners to "tune in" to the lesson.* **Performance Objectives** – *List learner objectives that meet the following criteria:* • *Behavior – what the learner is to "do"* • *Condition – under what circumstances the learner is to demonstrate the behavior* • *Standard – the degree of expertise the learner is to demonstrate*	
PRESENTATION	Notes (Safety; Strategies; What Worked, etc.)
Scope and Sequence – *Describe what will be taught and in what order.*	
APPLICATION	Notes (Safety; Strategies; What Worked, etc.)
Practice – *Describe what technical skill(s) learners are expected to perform, along with any other necessary information.* **Handouts** – *List any handouts/learning aids being used for instruction.* **Worksheets/Activities** – *List any worksheets/activities being used for instruction.*	
EVALUATION	Notes (Safety; Strategies; What Worked, etc.)
Formative* Assessments – *These assessments do not result in a grade, but do provide the instructor and learners with insight as to how well information is being comprehended (e.g., Q&A sessions; ungraded quizzes).* **Summative* Assessments** – *These assessments do result in a grade and may include quizzes, skill demonstrations, and homework assignments as well as tests.* ***All types of assessments need to connect to the lesson objectives.**	

Figure 3-2. A four-step standard format provides ease in following a lesson plan.

EVALUATE INSTRUCTIONAL MATERIALS

Instructional materials should always support the objectives and goals of the instructional program. There are many different types of instructional materials from which to choose. A few examples are textbooks, websites, technical manuals, related instructional media, and specialized tools and equipment.

All instructional materials and media such as PowerPoint® Presentations, videos, websites, charts, tables, and illustrations should be previewed prior to use. Printed materials should be selected carefully to ensure that the reading level is not beyond learner ability levels. There are numerous reliable readability formulas. These formulas are based on the premise that reading level is a function of the total number of words in a sentence and the number of multiple syllable words in a sentence. Reading level is reported as a reading grade level. The FORCAST readability formula is useful for assessing the readability level of technical materials because of its sensitivity to the large number of multiple syllable words often found in technical materials. **See Figure 3-3.**

FORCAST READABILITY FORMULA

1. Select a 150-word passage.

2. Count the number of one-syllable words in the passage (e.g., 90).

3. Divide that number by 10.

$$\frac{90}{10} = 9$$

4. Subtract the answer from 20.

$$20 - 9 = 11$$

This yields a readability level of grade 11, which means that individuals reading below the 11th grade level may have difficulty reading this material.

The formula may be written as follows:

$$20 - \frac{\text{number of one syllable words}}{10} = \text{Readability level}$$

Figure 3-3. The FORCAST readability formula can be used to assess the readability level of written materials.

A readability test is only one consideration in the selection process for written instructional materials. While selection of materials is somewhat subjective, the use of a rating scale lends a degree of objectivity by encouraging consistent evaluation. Criteria for choosing written instructional materials may include the following:

- content relevance
- technical accuracy
- up-to-date content
- cost
- style and size of type
- page layout and use of color
- use and appropriateness of graphics
- table of contents
- glossary, index, appendix, bibliography
- binding and quality of paper
- assessment activities
- supplementary materials (e.g., workbook, etc.)
- instructor resources

Develop Instruction Sheets for Exercises and Activities

Instructor-developed exercises and activities, along with those obtained from commercial sources, offer an opportunity for the instructor to apply specific concepts. The course format determines the amount of time available for exercises and activities. Instruction sheets are helpful and should be based on an analysis of the task to be performed or the knowledge to be acquired and the course objectives. Following is a list of various types of instruction sheets that help facilitate learning.

- Assignment sheets—These are a practical method for making individual and group assignments on readings and instructor-planned questions.
- Operation sheets—These are useful for performance-based outcomes. They provide step-by-step instructions for performing a specific skill or task.
- Job sheets—These list actions (performances) in proper sequence with sufficient detail to permit performance by learners.
- Information sheets—These are an efficient method for providing supplementary information to help learners meet knowledge-based objectives.

ORGANIZE AND UPDATE INSTRUCTIONAL MATERIALS

Instructors who use their time, energy, and resources wisely know that organization is the key to efficiency. Subject matter should be organized in terms of concepts, principles, and processes consistent with learner backgrounds and readiness to learn new information. Advance organizers such as instructor-prepared study guides and focused discussion questions encourage active participation and help to introduce and integrate new material and previously learned material.

Lesson plans can be easily modified for teaching, updating, and replacement as needed. Likewise, special instructional aids, props, models, etc., should be filed for safekeeping and easy access. Each time a lesson is taught, the instructor should review and evaluate materials and other resources based on the latest course objectives, learner needs, and technological changes.

SUMMARY

Effective instructors develop lessons and select and organize materials so that all learners have access to the instructional information. Each learner brings a unique experience, background, and set of talents to the learning situation. Conducting a pre-assessment of learner knowledge levels helps to identify the characteristics of each learner and provides valuable planning information to the instructor.

Instructor-developed exercises and activities allow learners to progress at their own rate by providing for individual differences. A course of study or instructional outline provides a comprehensive overview of the sequence of instructional lessons for the entire course. A detailed lesson plan written in a standard format provides a useful guide for instruction.

Lesson plans ensure that critical information is covered in the course, workshop, or seminar. Lessons should include enough material to allow for flexibility if the lesson proceeds more quickly or slowly than planned. Learner capabilities must also be addressed. The instructor may have advanced learners moving on to more complex activities, so attention can be directed to learners needing more assistance. In some instances, course content is based on selected units. If content areas are covered out of sequence, the instructor must present prerequisite information.

Self-Assessment Checklist

HINTS FOR THE HIGHLY EFFECTIVE INSTRUCTOR

INSTRUCTIONAL PLANNING

Yes	No	Needs Attention	
☐	☐	☐	1. Do you memorize the names of learners?
☐	☐	☐	2. Do you make sure that every learner is engaged in productive activity?
☐	☐	☐	3. Do you prepare a written lesson plan for each lesson ahead of time?
☐	☐	☐	4. Are your lesson plans filed for easy access and use?
☐	☐	☐	5. Do you begin your lessons with learner-centered objectives?
☐	☐	☐	6. Does each objective include an action word (behavior), the conditions for the performance behavior, and the criterion (standard) by which it will be measured?
☐	☐	☐	7. Do you include appropriate safety precautions in your lessons?
☐	☐	☐	8. Do you address learner differences between digital natives and digital immigrants?
☐	☐	☐	9. Do you plan ways to prepare and motivate your learners?
☐	☐	☐	10. Do you help learners develop positive work habits and attitudes?
☐	☐	☐	11. Do your lesson plans include techniques to help learners organize, synthesize, and integrate new information?
☐	☐	☐	12. Do you plan for learner participation, reinforcement, and practice?
☐	☐	☐	13. Do you provide learners opportunities for teamwork?
☐	☐	☐	14. Do you provide learners with feedback?
☐	☐	☐	15. Do you teach learners how to follow directions?
☐	☐	☐	16. Do your lesson plans include a reference section listing the instructional materials necessary for the lesson?
☐	☐	☐	17. Do you review each lesson plan for changes and corrections before it is presented?
☐	☐	☐	18. Do you select, prepare, and arrange supplementary learner materials?
☐	☐	☐	19. Do you organize your classroom/laboratory before each lesson begins?

INSTRUCTIONAL RESOURCES

A good instructor utilizes several instructional resources to present information and maximize comprehension. A variety of instructional resources can serve to maintain interest during long sessions. Like methods of instruction, the availability of instructional resources may be dependent on the facility, equipment, and/or budget.

RELEVANT REFERENCE MATERIALS

Reference material includes textbooks, periodicals, instructional manuals, trade journals, technical service bulletins, and company newsletters. User's manuals, technical journals, and industry standards can also be used as references throughout the course. In addition, many companies welcome the opportunity to have their company information distributed to potential customers. Industry and standards organizations can also be contacted for specific information.

The instructor should review references well in advance of instruction. Specific pages, websites, and printed resources may be bookmarked for future reference. Information should be easily accessed and presented in the context of the subject being taught.

INSTRUCTOR RESOURCE GUIDES

An instructor resource guide is a supplement to a textbook. An instructor resource guide often provides some or all of the following kinds of materials: PowerPoint® presentations, lesson plans, digital images, flash cards, test banks, answer keys, and additional references. In addition, suggestions for developing, organizing, and implementing instructional materials may be included in an instructor resource guide.

For a new instructor, the instructor resource guide provides a starting point for instruction. Experienced instructors can benefit as well from the variety of instructional options and teaching suggestions provided in an instructor resource guide.

Workbooks and Worksheets

Workbooks are designed for use with specific textbooks or instructional kits. Workbook activities apply specific principles and operations taught in the lesson and may require the use of the components included in an instructional kit. References to textbooks and required resources and kit components should be listed for each workbook activity. Answers for all or for selected activities are usually included in a separate answer key. The instructor should check copyright restrictions before duplicating and distributing commercially prepared digital and print materials.

Worksheets may serve as a catalyst for a discussion of content, a review of content, a formative assessment, or preparation for a test. Worksheets often accompany commercial instructional materials or may be developed by the instructor. Worksheets may be made available for download or reproduced prior to instruction. Depending on course needs, worksheets may be handed out to learners or used as an outline for class discussions. Worksheet answer keys should be obtained or developed.

Presentation Software

With presentation software, the instructor can use a variety of text, photographs, illustrations, video clips, audio clips, and other elements when delivering instruction. Navigational functions of some presentation software enable the instructor to select and enlarge images for greater emphasis. In addition, presentations created by the instructor allow photos and video clips of the specific training programs to be shown, which provides greater topical relevance. The presentation software product most commonly used for instruction is Microsoft® PowerPoint®.

Computer-Based Activities

Instructors have become increasingly reliant on computer software to support instruction. Computer-based activities vary in complexity from simple drill-and-practice programs to comprehensive, interactive simulations and games. Grade book software designed to keep records such as attendance, assignments, and grades is cost-efficient and timesaving. Learning management systems (LMSs) such as Blackboard® and Moodle® often integrate these capabilities.

The Internet

There are many instructional resources available on the Internet. Government publications are also available on the Internet. For example, current OSHA publications are available at the U.S. Government Printing Office (GPO) website. Product information is also available from many companies.

Instructors must evaluate Internet sites for accuracy, credibility, and relevance. They should verify that the subject matter is correct, with industry-specific terminology and safe processes and procedures. Other considerations include checking that the level of content is appropriate for learners. Finally, instructors should choose websites that are user friendly. **See Figure 4-1.**

WEBSITE EVALUATION

Site Title: _____ Date: _____

URL: _____

Directions: Using the following key, place a check (✓) in the blank opposite each item to assess each website element.

1 = Poor   2 = Average   3 = Above average   4 = Excellent

	1	2	3	4
Content				
• Accurate	___	___	___	___
• Timely	___	___	___	___
• Objective	___	___	___	___
• Relevant	___	___	___	___
• Organized	___	___	___	___
Links				
• Clearly defined	___	___	___	___
• Accessible	___	___	___	___
• Relevant	___	___	___	___
Graphics, Video, Sound				
• Relevant	___	___	___	___
• Download speed	___	___	___	___
Appearance				
• Attractive	___	___	___	___
• Clear	___	___	___	___

Figure 4-1. Instructors should evaluate websites for accuracy, credibility, and relevance.

Videos

Videos serve as a valuable teaching tool by presenting operations or activities that are difficult to replicate in an instructional setting. For example, troubleshooting equipment is well illustrated by showing footage of a typical application. An additional benefit of videos is that specific sections (clips) can be shown individually and/or repeatedly as required. Specific operations may also be videotaped by the instructor.

Online Learning

Many educational programs offer online learning so that courses can be made available to a wider range of learners. When onsite attendance is difficult due to geographical limitations or due to responsibilities that limit a learner's participation in traditional instruction, online learning is particularly beneficial.

Instructors who provide online learning may use a variety of options such as video conferencing, chat functions, or virtual whiteboards. Social media such as Twitter®, Instagram®, YouTube®, Facebook®, and blogs are excellent ways to connect with learners and individualize learning experiences. Digital natives are especially adept at using social media.

Online learning can be as effective as onsite instruction if proper preparations are made. Course requirements and lesson objectives should be planned carefully. Learner needs, along with learner access to required technology, should be assessed before any technology is selected. For example, streaming video or immersive simulations may require high-speed Internet access.

Furthermore, chat functions help facilitate communication and reinforce learning. Such strategies provide timely feedback on learner progress and contribute to positive learning. Strategies that promote and support learning where interaction occurs outside the scheduled class time (asynchronous communication) such as email and discussion boards supplement instructional activities.

Finally, depending on a variety of administrative and logistical requirements, online learning may be blended with onsite instruction. For example, courses that include hands-on laboratory exercises may require learners to report periodically to a lab to complete assignments. Also, tests may need to be taken at a proctored testing site.

Copyrighted Versus Public Domain Material

Instructors must use a variety of reference material to support the content presented in a course. This includes the use of copyrighted reference material. Copyright is the legal ownership of literary, musical, or artistic work that authorizes the right to reproduce, publish, and/or sell the work. Copyright is indicated on a work by the word copyright or the symbol ©, the name of the copyright holder, and the year.

Additional statements may be used to further define limitations for reproduction. The phrase "All rights reserved" is commonly used to specify all derivative use of the work.

Instructors must understand and follow federal legislation related to copyrighted material. The Copyright Revision Act of 1976 is the fourth comprehensive revision of the copyright law. Copyright not only protects authors and publishers, but also benefits society from the creative efforts that are protected. Copyright laws vary in different countries. Copyrighted material may be reproduced within the bounds of fair use for instructional purposes. Reproduction of copyrighted material beyond fair use is illegal.

Permission to reproduce copyrighted material must be requested in writing from the copyright holder. Information in the request should include the definition of material to be reproduced, the manner in which material is to be used, and the number of copies to be made.

The copyright holder will assess the request for the impact on the copyright holder and/or author, impact on the market for the material, and the value of the copyrighted material reproduced. The copyright holder has the right to grant or deny permission to reproduce the copyrighted material and to charge a fee for the use of copyrighted materials.

Some reference material is in the public domain. The public domain is a term used to describe "property of the public." Public domain material is free from copyright restrictions. For example, material published by the United States government is public domain material. The instructor and instructional institution are best served by using careful consideration when reproducing copyrighted material.

PRIMARY SOURCE INFORMATION

Instructors should take care to reference primary sources of information from which copyrighted or public domain material is taken. Primary sources are unaltered, original documents that were created at the time the actions or events took place. Primary sources come in many forms; however, the technical instructor will mostly be concerned with industry standards, government regulations, and applicable codes. In general, the instructor must be sure that the source information is complete, accurate, and up-to-date. Local libraries, professional organizations, and publishers provide access to a host of primary sources related to technical education.

The Internet can be useful for locating primary sources. Using specific rather than broad terms facilitates a more efficient search. For example, in a search for the Americans with Disabilities Act (ADA), typing in "Americans with Disabilities Act" in a search engine will result in more than 1000 references. It will then be necessary to select the most reliable source, which should be the actual legislation in the federal statutes. In this case, an instructor may choose to reference the ADA home page, which provides numerous links to specific parts of the act. In general, websites with a nonbiased, balanced approach to presenting primary sources are more reliable than sites where the source material is used to persuade readers to a particular point of view.

Instructors should take care to provide complete information about primary sources regardless of where they are located. Complete information is necessary, not only to give credit to the source, but also to permit the instructor and learners to locate the source if needed. Basic information to include on a reference list are the title and author of the document or book or the developer of the website, name of the publisher, place, year, volume number, federal code, the URL, and the date. Instructors may choose to put the information in an order they deem most useful to learners.

Instructional Tool Kits

Instructional tool kits include special components, tools, and supplies needed for laboratory exercises. Instructional tool kits may be available from a commercial vendor, or the instructor may create them. The best instruction employs hands-on practice on components and related equipment found in the field.

Instructional tool kits may be reused. However, the instructor must ensure that the kits have all the components and that the components are safe and operational. The instructor should maintain a spare tool kit for replacement of damaged or missing components.

Training Stations

Training stations allow hands-on activities on actual or simulated equipment. Training stations usually permit a variety of tasks to be performed in less space than the actual equipment in industry. Instructors can develop training stations. For example, a security alarm system training station can be constructed with system components mounted on a display board. This allows representation and access to all system components that would normally be located in different parts of a building.

Tools and Equipment

Tools and equipment used in the instructional program must be in good working order and representative of that found in industry. The instructor should check tools and equipment for safe and proper operating condition. For example, tools should be accurately calibrated, safety guards should be in place and fit properly, and fuses and safety interlocks should be in good working condition. Replacement parts must be available when needed. Some parts are expensive, and precautions should be taken to avoid unnecessary wear and tear in order to reduce the number of replacement parts needed.

SAFETY INFORMATION

Safety information is the most important information conveyed by the instructor. The instructor must identify potential risks and minimize the potential for injury and equipment damage. Some activities involve greater risk than others. For example, measuring AC voltage at a wall outlet has a greater potential for injury than measuring DC voltage in a flashlight battery. Safety knowledge and practices cannot be overemphasized.

Safety hazards vary with different activities. Tool and equipment manufacturers provide safety precautions and procedures to help the instructor reduce hazards that could lead to an accident. Safety hazards also vary depending on the facility used. For example, a seminar presented in a hotel conference center may pose fewer safety hazards than an instructional setting within a production facility.

The instructor should be aware that tools and equipment from different manufacturers might not have the same safety features. In addition, some testing equipment may be damaged from previous use. Depending on the instructional program, it may be the responsibility of the learner to provide a test tool. The instructor must not assume that test tools brought to the course are in safe operating condition. All tools, equipment, and related accessories must be tested before instruction begins. The lesson plan should also include warnings, safety precautions, and emergency procedures. The instructor may include additional notes as necessary.

BUSINESS AND INDUSTRY RELATIONSHIPS

The link between technical instruction and business and industry practices is critical for success. Most employers are willing and eager to be involved in instructional programs. An active advisory committee should be established to provide program guidance and identify potential job opportunities for participants in the instructional course or program.

Local business and industry representatives can provide real-life examples for learners through group tours, practical experiences, presentations, and demonstrations. In addition, equipment and material contributions from business and industry can greatly enhance technical instruction.

SUMMARY

The instructor may select resources from print and digital media to supplement and enhance learner experiences. Internet resources, textbooks, workbooks, instructor resource guides, instructional tool kits, technical manuals, worksheets, videos, and online learning provide content practice, review, and assessment of comprehension of material presented during instruction. Unlike material in the public domain, the instructor must obtain written permission to reproduce copyrighted material.

The Internet is a tremendous resource and instructional tool that can offer additional resources. The information available is similar to walking into a huge library; the desired information is somewhere in the library but must be located. The instructor should provide specific direction to maximize the benefits to learners.

Computer proficiency is a prerequisite for success in virtually every occupation. The instructor should include content and activities in the course that require the use of relevant computer applications. The instructor should also serve as a role model for using these computer applications.

The instructional program should serve as a model for safe work practices. The instructor must demonstrate all safety practices and procedures to be followed. In addition, the instructor is responsible for maintaining a safe learning environment.

Involving business and industry representatives adds technical validity to the course. Their expertise benefits learners as well as reinforces the need for technical training.

Self-Assessment Checklist

HINTS FOR THE HIGHLY EFFECTIVE INSTRUCTOR

INSTRUCTIONAL RESOURCES

Yes	No	Needs Attention	
☐	☐	☐	1. Do you use up-to-date technical materials and supplies?
☐	☐	☐	2. Do you use articles that present innovations in your technical area?
☐	☐	☐	3. Do you maintain an up-to-date library for your program?
☐	☐	☐	4. Do you use an instructor's guide?
☐	☐	☐	5. Do you assign online activities to learners?
☐	☐	☐	6. Do you use computer programs to manage instruction?
☐	☐	☐	7. Do you use workbooks and/or worksheets?
☐	☐	☐	8. Do you use the Internet to find instructional resources?
☐	☐	☐	9. Do you encourage learners to use the Internet to seek information?
☐	☐	☐	10. Do you use a variety of visual media to supplement instruction?
☐	☐	☐	11. Do you understand copyright law?
☐	☐	☐	12. Do you set up learner training stations?
☐	☐	☐	13. Do you test all equipment to ensure that it is in good working order?
☐	☐	☐	14. Do you repeatedly encourage safety in handling tools and equipment?
☐	☐	☐	15. Do you use visuals to review key points of your lecture?
☐	☐	☐	16. Do you use instructional tool kits to give learners hands-on practice?
☐	☐	☐	17. Do you ensure that all components within instructional tool kits are in safe operating condition?
☐	☐	☐	18. Do you encourage local business and industry to become involved with your instructional program?
☐	☐	☐	19. Do you encourage the development of online learning?
☐	☐	☐	20. Are you aware of differences in safety features of tools and equipment from different manufacturers?

INSTRUCTIONAL METHODS

5

HINTS FOR THE HIGHLY EFFECTIVE INSTRUCTOR

Instructional methods vary with the learners and the content areas covered. The best instruction occurs through the use of several instructional methods. In addition, an effective instructor can quickly sense which instructional methods are the most and least effective in a given situation. In some cases, the instructional method may be limited by time, facilities, equipment, and/or budget. This challenges the instructor to be more creative.

GAIN AND HOLD LEARNER ATTENTION

Valuable time is wasted if an instructor attempts to teach without first securing the attention of all learners in the class. The instructor needs to create an environment in which learners are motivated to learn. Explaining the importance and relevance of a lesson helps bring meaning to the information and creates a positive attitude toward learning. It is easier to sustain the attention and interest of learners when they are actively involved in their learning.

The instructor should clearly communicate the intended outcomes and expectations of the lesson. The instructor should also explain the relevance of the current lesson in context with material presented previously and information yet to be covered. Information about safety procedures and precautions should be emphasized.

Learners should be challenged but not overwhelmed in an instructional program. A pace that maintains a variety of learner activity and adequate challenge is desirable. Breaks during instruction are necessary to maintain learner alertness. The instructor also needs occasional breaks to maintain instructional vitality.

USE THE FOUR-STEP METHOD OF INSTRUCTION

The four-step method of instruction–*planning, preparation, presentation, and evaluation*–is a straightforward and effective method for delivering instruction. In the *planning* step, instructors should keep in mind the importance of matching instruction with the learning styles and preferences of the learners and develop a lesson plan and corresponding handouts that are well thought out. This will help ensure that lesson objectives are appropriate and consistent with individual learner needs and abilities.

The *preparation* step involves getting learners ready to learn by providing an orientation to the lesson. This may be accomplished by providing a brief overview of the lesson, asking preplanned questions before the lesson, or assigning a chapter in the textbook or problems as homework before they are to be discussed. The planning and preparation steps help to guide the presentation step.

For the *presentation* step, the instructor must decide the scope and sequence of the content being presented and which delivery methods will best serve learner needs and accomplish the lesson objectives. Lecture, demonstration, or group or individualized instruction may be used alone or in combination. For example, if the lesson objective is to impart knowledge related to the theory of hydraulics, the lecture-discussion method is an appropriate delivery mode; whereas the demonstration method is more effective for a lesson designed to teach the correct procedure for taking blood pressure.

Instructor interest and enthusiasm for the subject is readily apparent to learners. The manner in which information is presented affects comprehension. The instructor sets the standard for the way information is disseminated and how the class is expected to respond. Key points listed in the instructional outline should serve as a guide to the scope and sequence of content. **See Figure 5-1.** References should be available for use as information is presented.

Evaluation is the final step of instruction. *Evaluation* is a method through which the instructor measures learner achievement of the knowledge, skills, and attitudes covered in a course. The purpose of evaluation is to provide a basis for grades or advancement to the next course. Evaluation requires professional judgment regarding the adequacy of a learner's knowledge, understanding, skills, and attitudes. Evaluations are typically categorized as formative or summative.

A *formative evaluation* is a form of assessment that is used to identify inadequacies in terms of learner knowledge, skill, or attitudes during the instructional program. For example, questions or quizzes interjected during the instructional sequence can give learners an opportunity to clarify their own level of understanding. Formative evaluations can also identify competencies that learners have mastered, allowing the instructional process to eliminate needless duplication of content. Learners who have successful experiences with formative evaluations during the instructional sequence feel more positive toward learning.

Evaluation of learning at the conclusion of a course is referred to as summative evaluation. A *summative evaluation* is a form of assessment that ascertains the extent to which learners have achieved the established objectives of the instructional program. Scores on written tests and performance tests as well as grades on projects and reports are forms of summative evaluation for a course.

SCOPE AND SEQUENCE	
LESSON PLAN #86	
PREPARATION	Notes
Scope and Sequence – *Describe what will be taught and in what order.*	
1. Review the objectives of today's lesson. (5 min.)	*Provide learners with the objectives in written form (on the whiteboard, online via the LMS, or as a handout).*
2. Explain that today the class will be reviewing content in preparation for the written portion of the exam and that tomorrow's lesson will focus on practicing for the performance portion of the exam. (5 min.)	*Remind learners that knowing and following safety protocols will be part of the written and performance portions of the exam.*
3. Divide learners into two teams. Allow the teams a couple of minutes to select a team name. Write a team name on each side of the board and ask the members of each team to form a line five feet away from the side of the board that bears their team name. Hand a marker to the person at the front of the line of each team. Explain that when a review question is asked, the two people who have the marker are to go to the board and write down the answer. The team that writes the correct answer first gets a point. The marker is then handed to the next person in line. Each member of the team will get the opportunity to answer a question. The winning team will be given five-minutes of extra time to complete the performance portion of the exam. (35 min.)	*Remind learners that games can be an effective way to learn and remember information that may be on the exam.*
4. Pass back the graded study questions. Have each student choose a partner and have them quiz each other on the key terms in the chapter. (10 min.)	*Remind learners to study the questions that they missed.*
5. Close the lesson by reminding learners to be prepared to practice for the performance portion of the exam tomorrow. (5 min.)	*Remind learners that appropriate PPE will be required tomorrow.*

Figure 5-1. The instructor must decide the scope and sequence of the content being presented and which delivery methods will best serve learner needs and accomplish the lesson objectives.

INTEGRATE READING, WRITING, AND MATHEMATICS

Reading, writing, and mathematics are as important today as they have ever been. Failure to include opportunities for learners to enhance these fundamental skills puts them at a disadvantage in terms of employment.

There is a perception that learners in technical courses may not be interested in reading, writing, and mathematics. The technical instructor should not accept this perception and instead expect learners to achieve competency in these subjects. Also, learners are more receptive to mastering these subjects when the instructor ties them directly to applications of the technical content of the instructional program.

The instructor should provide learners with and show examples of reading material in their occupational area such as trade magazines, newsletters, catalogs, bulletins, and technical manuals.

ENCOURAGE THINKING, DOING, AND LEARNING

The importance of learning to think cannot be overestimated. The technical worker must adapt to rapidly changing conditions and demands. Skill of hand is necessary and important, but the ability to retrieve, analyze, and use information in the workplace is critical for success. Thinking is an internal process that may manifest itself in overt and observable behavior, and habits of thinking are acquired by practice.

It is not unusual for learners to come into an instructional program with learned habits. It is much easier to learn correct habits than to unlearn incorrect habits. Therefore, one of the most difficult yet important responsibilities of the instructor is to serve as a role model by demonstrating good habits. This is one reason, aside from safety concerns, that instructors should talk through the steps of a process or procedure during a demonstration. This technique helps learners understand and practice correct processes and procedures.

Thinking as a means of learning is an important concept. Learning requires forming new associations based on previously learned information and prior experiences. For example, when an instructor helps learners understand the relationship between an instructional lecture and a laboratory experiment, learners see how to apply theory to practical situations. Thus the thinking process becomes clearer, and learning is facilitated.

PREPARE LECTURES

Lecture is an instructional method that uses oral presentation of information to a group. Lecture is an efficient method of quickly disseminating information. Information is conveyed in a one-directional mode. The primary advantage of lecture is the ability to impact many learners at a given time.

PREPARE DEMONSTRATIONS

Demonstration is an instructional method that provides an opportunity for the instructor to present or perform skills required in the field. Demonstrations teach proper technique as tools, materials, or instruments are manipulated. The demonstration method is particularly useful for presenting hands-on techniques.

The instructor must prepare for the demonstration in advance to reduce the possibility of errors in performance. A camcorder and large screens may be required to permit visual access to the movements being demonstrated. Using the demonstration method generally promotes learner interest.

DESIGN HANDS-ON ACTIVITIES

A hands-on activity is an instructional method that uses physical contact and interaction during a given procedure. Hands-on activities integrate auditory and visual senses with touch to produce greater comprehension. Hands-on activities that use experimentation can produce valuable learning experiences. Expected results can serve to confirm a theory or principle; unexpected results can serve to elicit curiosity and critical thinking about the causes.

The instructor can also use hands-on activities to stimulate critical thinking skills. For example, providing selected members of the class with equipment that has a defective component or a component with an incorrect rating can spur a discussion regarding the cause of the problem and the troubleshooting steps required.

PROMOTE ONLINE LEARNING

Online learning provides additional opportunities for individuals to access information and practice skills. Online learning allows the instructor to post discussion topics, problems, and assignments within a learning management system (LMS) and allows individual learners to access that information at their own convenience. Learners provide their responses and the instructor provides feedback.

Online courses often have chat rooms set aside for interactions between instructors and learners, or between learners and peer learners. Instructors should be directly involved in determining how parts of existing instructional programs can be delivered online effectively.

Online learning has versatility and economic advantages. Companies may develop their own online infrastructures and content, or they may employ a technology professional or consultant to assist in establishing online instruction and to train instructors to conduct and manage instruction.

Many courses are also available as massive open online courses (MOOCs). A MOOC is an online course that allows unlimited participation from learners via the Internet. MOOCs are organized courses developed for free access anytime.

Typical online course content and features such as video lectures, chat functions, and forums provide instruction to thousands of learners interested in specific courses or curricula. Many universities now offer MOOCs, in addition to other providers such as Khan Academy®, edX®, Coursera®, and UDACITY®. Enrollments in MOOCs are quite high. However, completion rates are usually around 13% to 15%. MOOCs offer a low-cost alternative to traditional academic institutions and are expected to grow with the demand for educational opportunities.

USE EDUCATIONAL GAMES

Another way to reinforce learning is through the use of educational games. An educational game is a computer game that has a purpose other than entertainment. In an instructional setting, educational games are designed to achieve learning outcomes using simulations or other activities in a computer game environment. Educational games can provide engaging learning experiences using scenarios common to course topics. For example, when teaching electrical safety, there are several games available that test the ability to identify the proper personal protective equipment to be used in locations with electrical hazards.

With educational games, learners are required to use their thinking, planning, and technical skills and learn through doing and guided discovery. Educational games can be used as part of a course to test comprehension and critical-thinking skills or as a self-study reinforcement activity for concepts presented in the course. Scores earned by individual learners can be used as motivation to increase proficiency. Team play can be used to develop teamwork and collaborative solutions. Educational games will continue to increase in value as technology and game designs evolve.

DEVELOP TARGETED LEARNER RESOURCES

Content curation is the process of finding, classifying, organizing, sorting, and presenting relevant information for an instructional program. Content curation is much like curation in a museum where an individual known as a curator or archivist selects, organizes, stores, and retrieves documents, objects, materials, and artifacts for the purpose of later use.

Time spent planning instruction is maximized with content curation, because curating content reduces the time an instructor must spend developing original materials for each specific topic or concept taught. When curation is integrated into daily (or weekly) planning, instructors can easily retrieve, modify, and share information. Curation allows instructors to put information in context for future use. Almost 80% of content that is shared is curated and only about 20% is original. Original materials are important, useful, and necessary for certain situations. However, there is no need to reinvent the wheel.

It may be possible for instructors to develop their own system of curation; however, such a system is not recommended, as it would be quickly outdated, incomplete, hard to manage, and overall inefficient. Curation software is available with special curation tools that will select accurate and relevant information on the web for a specific topic. The curation process interprets information from the web to ensure that the information is the best available on a topic and classified correctly. Curation tools locate, organize, and store similar content in one space.

Free curation software is available to assist instructors and others with their search and collection efforts. For example, Scoop.it® offers a free account for individuals to curate up to five topics. The curated items can be posted to Facebook, Twitter, or other social media. It is easy to sign up for a free account on several of the curation sites. For example, to sign up for Scoop.it, a name, email address, and password is all that is required. Scoop.it assigns a URL to each member.

Content curation is a way to enhance instructional materials and foster mutual promotion of shared content. Shared information encourages and facilitates networking and can lead to better-informed instructors and learners.

USE TECHNOLOGY TO AID COMPREHENSION

Effective instructors use technology to aid learner understanding and comprehension. One method that is gaining increased popularity is the development and maintenance of course websites. A course website allows learners to access course information and instructional materials via the Internet at their convenience and when the need arises. Initial development of a website requires time and planning on the part of the instructor. However, after the site is up and running, the instructor need only maintain and update the posted information.

The home page for the website might include permanent information about the course, as well as information that may change periodically, such as due dates for projects or quizzes. Links can be provided that allow learners to download course materials such as the course syllabus, study guides, and PowerPoint® slides. One of the greatest benefits of an instructor-developed website is that the instructor can preview and evaluate the accuracy and timeliness of on-line articles related to the subject matter before providing hyperlinks to the articles. A course website is an excellent way to serve learners whose work schedules may not permit them to access the information in traditional ways.

Videos can also be powerful instructional tools used to supplement instruction. There are many commercially prepared educational videos on the market that provide a good starting point for beginning instructors. Another source for instructional videos is YouTube®. YouTube is an Internet video-sharing service that provides access to videos posted by other users. The instructor must carefully vet videos for accuracy and provide links for easy access in the instructional setting.

If appropriate and relevant videos or DVDs are not available, instructors can produce their own videos with a digital video camera. Costs for video equipment have gone down, and there are many features available that simplify the development of instructional videos. In addition, smartphones can also be used to record digital video.

Using real-time demonstrations or storyboards, the instructor can select relevant video segments, edit, or add sound and other special effects to create unique and relevant instructional materials. Videos can be as brief as a few seconds or as lengthy as several minutes. In addition, videos can be used to enhance instruction in PowerPoint® presentations or used as resources in online-delivered courses.

Have Learners Participate in Job Shadowing

Job shadowing is an instructional method in which the learner is assigned to one or more successful employees at a company to observe the employee performing daily job duties. Many companies allow "shadowing" of employees so that learners can gain firsthand experience. The shadowing time may be for one day, one week, or longer.

By observing one or more employees for an extended period of time, learners can get an idea about specific job duties and learn state-of-the-art procedures. An added benefit of job shadowing is the opportunity for learners to ask questions of experts at the time the questions arise.

Bring in Guest Speakers

Guest speakers used in instructional programs offer perspectives that enhance the content presented. Guest speakers can be chosen from manufacturers, local companies, product service facilities, and suppliers. For example, an electrical equipment distributor can provide current information about new products and capabilities.

Take Learners on Industry Tours

Industry tours provide an opportunity to leave the instructional facility and experience related content-area activities on-site. Instructors should be aware that industry tours require additional planning for transportation and coordination of the host visitation site. Some locations may require personal protective equipment such as eye and head protection.

Prior to the tour, the instructor should explain what will be seen and how it relates to the material covered in class. After the tour, the instructor should review and summarize the information presented during the tour. The instructor should be knowledgeable of personal and institutional liabilities and follow all precautions when taking learners on industry tours.

Attend Seminars and Conferences

Technical seminar programs by recognized companies present new products, tools, and equipment. Conferences offer a wealth of new information from industry professionals and equipment vendors. Whenever appropriate and possible, instructors should participate in technical seminars and conferences and encourage learners to participate as well.

Conference presenters often provide special handouts or software of their presentations. These kinds of resources can be valuable teaching tools for later review and discussion. Other ways to acquire information include reading trade publications, attending classes, and participating in professional organizations. Conferences also provide opportunities to share common problems and solutions with peer professionals.

Promote Cooperative Learning

Cooperative learning uses the collective efforts of several learners to acquire new information. This method is particularly useful when there is a broad range of knowledge and experience in the group. Cooperative learning requires interaction among all learners in the group. The members of the group may be preselected to ensure a variety of individual competencies. Educational games can be used to foster cooperative learning.

Establish a Learning Community

A learning community (LC) is a group of learners who share the common goal of mastering instructional content and come together to share individual experiences, resources, and expertise. Instructional content may be for a specific course, more than one course, or an entire program. The benefit of LCs is the supportive and collaborative nature of a group in which each learner is responsible for the learning of every other learner in the group.

For example, an LC may be formed when learners are required to have prerequisite knowledge before they can move forward to the next level or course. Prerequisite knowledge might include the ability to apply certain codes, make calculations, perform computer operations, or interpret data. After the prerequisite knowledge is mastered, the LC can continue to master new information. An LC is more than a group of learners who meet informally from time-to-time as a study group. A true LC is a structured group that requires a time commitment on the part of instructors and learners.

The most effective LC includes at least one instructor and several learners who are committed to the process and goals of shared learning. This means that the group meets regularly over a sustained period of time at a predetermined location during a scheduled time for a common purpose. Instructors should take the lead in forming an LC. Instructors identify learning goals, schedules, and expectations in consultation with learners. After the LC is formed, an instructor participates as a contributing member of the group with shared responsibilities rather than directing the group. Learners, as well as instructors, facilitate the group interactions.

LCs continue to gain popularity as a way to integrate instructional content with learning, individual and social responsibility, and instructor-learner relationships. Research shows that learners who participate in a learning community demonstrate enhanced learning and persistence in their instructional program.

Participate in Team Instruction

Team instruction is an instructional method that involves the use of more than one instructor. Team instruction can offer the advantage of combined industrial and instructional experience. This can provide a richer instructional experience for the learners. Team instruction also allows an instructor to focus on a particular topic. For example, one instructor may be responsible for special features of some equipment, and the other instructor may be responsible for representative applications in the field.

Incorporate Problem Solving

Problem solving uses an instructor-created problem to elicit logical reasoning to find a solution. Problem solving should be used only with learners who possess knowledge of basic concepts, principles, and procedures. For example, an advanced activity could include common problems contributing to electric motor failure. Knowledge of electrical theory, troubleshooting techniques, and contributing causes is required before determining the cause of motor failure. Problem-solving activities must be selected carefully to ensure that they are appropriate for all learners.

The first step in problem solving is to identify and clarify the problem. For example, specific tasks to be accomplished or decisions to be made can pose problems. Learners should know how to state the problem in writing and formulate a separate statement for each problem. After the problem has been stated, it should be analyzed to ascertain the relevant facts, circumstances, or conditions surrounding the problem. It is usually necessary to obtain new information about the problem.

Next, possible solutions should be written. Then, the advantages, disadvantages, and direct and indirect consequences of each possible solution should be listed. The most appropriate and feasible solution should be selected, and the solution should then be implemented.

Finally, learners should evaluate the solution and decide if the desired results were obtained. If the results are correct, appropriate, and desired, then the facts were correct and adequate, and the thinking was sound. If undesirable outcomes result, the problem-solving process should be repeated, taking care to clarify the problem statement and gather information that may have been omitted.

Use Worksheets

Having learners complete worksheets serves as a checkpoint of comprehension. Depending on the purpose of the worksheets and the type of questions, special references, tools, and equipment may be necessary to complete the worksheets. For example, learners might need to use the textbook to find the answers to worksheet questions. Worksheets can also function as quizzes. The instructor should collect the worksheets for documentation as needed.

Employ Questioning Techniques

Questions are an important part of the learning process and help to correct errors, clarify concepts and procedures, expand learner knowledge, and monitor and assess learner progress. Questions can be derived from each instructional unit and can function as a guide for review as well as indicators of learner comprehension.

The instructor must attract the attention of the class before asking questions or it will be necessary to repeat the questions. Habitual repetition of questions or learners' answers for the sake of those who are not paying attention wastes valuable instructional time and may eventually help develop an attitude of indifference on the part of learners and frustration on the part of the instructor.

Questions should be stated clearly and distinctly so that all learners can hear and understand them. If additional time is available, questions can be used to lead into discussion of related content areas.

Calling a learner's name before a question is posed often results in some learners losing interest. The instructor should state the question first, and then call on a learner to answer, so that all members of the group are required to think about the question. Volunteer answers should be accepted only under the control of the instructor. It is better to call on a specific learner so that group recitation is discouraged. Learners who do not know the answer can give the appearance of knowing when the class answers in unison.

Questioning learners in rotation is not the best technique. It indicates who is to answer next and relieves the rest of the learners of the need to listen and think about the answer. The instructor may glance at a seating chart or select roll cards arbitrarily to call on learners. The best method is to learn learners' names as soon as possible. Questions should be stated to avoid "yes" or "no" responses. Questions should be framed so that learners are required to summarize information or explain why, how, under what conditions, and to what extent.

Use Visual Aids

Visualization is one of the most effective ways to learn. Real objects, models, and cutaways are excellent aids to use during demonstrations. When these are not available, simulations, videos, or illustrations may be used.

Instructional aids should be prepared or secured before the class begins to maximize class time and hold learner interest. All whiteboards should be free of illustrations, notes, formulas, and other information left from the previous lesson. Extraneous information or objects that distract the attention of learners should also be removed.

Safety precautions should be demonstrated and explained thoroughly. Failure to explain and demonstrate the proper operation of a tool or piece of equipment can lead to breakage as well as loss of instructional time.

Assign Learner Presentations

Learner presentations compel learners to acquire a comprehensive understanding of content. This is especially true if a question and answer session is included after each presentation. Insightful questions can arise from the group, and the presenter must be prepared to answer each question adequately. Learner presentations also provide opportunities for advanced investigation into a specific content area.

Individualize Instruction

Individualized instruction is designed to meet the specific learning needs and ability level of an individual learner. Few instructional programs have the resources to provide total individualized instruction. However, an instructor can use prepackaged instructional modules to meet the specific needs of learners. For example, a learner with less field experience than the rest of the class may require additional individualized demonstrations of a particular technique.

Assign Homework

A reasonable amount of homework reinforces learning through review of previously learned material, helps prepare learners for further learning, and provides a method of assessing learner progress. The instructor should provide guidance in locating resources to help learners complete homework assignments. Every assignment should require learners to apply concepts in a valid activity.

Homework assignments should be explained fully, along with the date when the assignment is due. Learners should be required to turn assignments in on time. Only extenuating circumstances as determined by the instructor should permit learners to deviate from the due date. Any penalty for late assignments should be communicated to learners before the assignment is due. Every assignment should be evaluated and returned by the next class meeting with appropriate feedback.

USE BLENDED LEARNING STRATEGIES

Effective instructors use blended learning strategies by incorporating a variety of teaching and delivery methods to accommodate different learning styles. Online delivery is best suited for instruction in subject areas that do not require hands-on activities using tools and/or equipment. Instructor-led delivery provides face-to-face interaction and activities associated with traditional classroom or lab settings. Blended learning is the integration of online delivery with instructor-led delivery to maximize the benefits of each.

A major advantage of blended learning is the flexibility in how instruction is delivered. For example, in the past homework was commonly reviewed in class or graded by the instructor. Using a learning management system (LMS), the homework is completed online and graded automatically. This frees up valuable class time and increases the instructor-led time for important hands-on and face-to-face activities only available on-site. Practice of skills in a supervised environment can be conducted with immediate on-site interaction. Variations of blended learning can be used to provide the most valuable instructional experience for learners in a specific course or program.

GIVE COMPREHENSIVE DIRECTIONS

Learners need to understand assignments and the instructor's expectations. Learners should be given an opportunity to think about the process of completing an assignment, and they should understand clearly what has been assigned. Properly prepared instruction sheets can help explain how to carry out specific assignments.

SUMMARY

Effective instructors use a variety of instructional methods and supplementary information during instruction. The method used should be determined by the purpose, objectives, and goals of the lesson as well as by the learners' needs. The instructor can provide personal experience and insight, examples of the ways in which information is used in the field, and information about the application of the subject matter in the workplace.

The amount of time available for a particular subject or lesson may influence the mode of delivery. For example, online learning may be an option when some instruction can be delivered via an LMS. Lessons should include enough material to allow for flexibility if the lesson proceeds more quickly or slowly than planned.

Learner capabilities must also be addressed when selecting an instructional method. The instructor may move advanced learners on to more complex activities so attention can be directed to learners needing more assistance. In some instances, course content can be presented through individualized instruction modules.

If content areas are covered out of sequence, the instructor must review prerequisite information. If time permits, additional activities can be developed or selected to enhance understanding or provide more hands-on tasks.

Learners will be better prepared to learn if the instructor explains a lesson before assigning it. After the lesson, a review of the important points helps fix the lesson objectives in learners' minds. Likewise, the lesson preview and review make it easier for the instructor to teach the current lesson and prepare for the next lesson.

Instructional skill, like any skill, improves with practice. Instructors acquire many instructional skills through trial and error and by emulating successful instructors. Courses that cover learning theory and instructional methods are also helpful in acquiring and enhancing instructional skill.

Self-Assessment Checklist

HINTS FOR THE HIGHLY EFFECTIVE INSTRUCTOR

INSTRUCTIONAL METHODS

Yes	No	Needs Attention	
☐	☐	☐	1. Do you use a variety of teaching methods?
☐	☐	☐	2. Do you demonstrate the use of tools and equipment?
☐	☐	☐	3. Do you use a variety of hands-on activities?
☐	☐	☐	4. Do you invite business and industry representatives to speak to learners?
☐	☐	☐	5. Do you participate in seminars and conferences?
☐	☐	☐	6. Do your learners participate in seminars and conferences?
☐	☐	☐	7. Do you individualize instruction?
☐	☐	☐	8. Do you assign homework?
☐	☐	☐	9. Do you review homework assignments promptly?
☐	☐	☐	10. Do you talk through the processes that you are demonstrating?
☐	☐	☐	11. Do you encourage class discussions among learners?
☐	☐	☐	12. Do you use instructional techniques that enhance learners' critical-thinking and problem-solving skills?
☐	☐	☐	13. Do you plan questions for each lesson topic and include these in your lesson plans?
☐	☐	☐	14. Do you ask questions that require learners to describe, explain, or solve a problem?
☐	☐	☐	15. Do you encourage learners to read?
☐	☐	☐	16. Do you encourage learners to write?
☐	☐	☐	17. Do you encourage learners to ask questions?
☐	☐	☐	18. Do you encourage learners to use mathematics?
☐	☐	☐	19. Are your instructional materials up-to-date?
☐	☐	☐	20. Do you use pictures, charts, cutaways, and real tools and equipment in your instruction?
☐	☐	☐	21. Do you prepare and organize materials, tools, and equipment before you conduct a demonstration?

LEARNING ENVIRONMENT ORGANIZATION 6

HINTS FOR THE HIGHLY EFFECTIVE INSTRUCTOR

Well-organized, safe, and positive classrooms and laboratories are prerequisites to effective teaching and learning. Classroom and laboratory situations and challenges differ with each instructor and group of learners. There are, however, some basic strategies for organizing and maintaining the learning environment that help to ensure high levels of learning and learner satisfaction.

ESTABLISH CLASSROOM AND LABORATORY RULES AND PROCEDURES

Learners want to know what is expected of them in terms of work and behavior. Rules, procedures, and expectations related to classroom and laboratory behavior should be established at the beginning of each course. Classroom rules provide structure and a consistent learning environment. Classroom and laboratory procedures are important because they often relate to safety, emergency situations such as severe weather conditions and evacuation, and general institutional policies. Instructor expectations of learners regarding rules and procedures set clear boundaries and establish a safe learning environment.

Rules should be limited in number. It is more effective to develop a few rules and enforce them consistently and fairly than to develop a lot of rules that may be easily forgotten. Also, rules developed with learner input help to create and maintain a positive learning environment. Learners respect an instructor who enforces rules that they helped develop.

The procedures followed for a course or program should be based on safe technical practices used in industry. Good habits formed in instructional programs carry over to the workplace. For example, procedures for cleaning and organizing a laboratory at the end of an instructional session must be clearly defined. The procedures should be posted and a copy provided to each learner. The consequences of not following the procedures should also be explained.

CREATE AN ACTIVE AND POSITIVE LEARNING ENVIRONMENT

A positive learning environment is one in which all learners feel free to participate, ask and answer questions, and put forth ideas without being ridiculed or embarrassed by the instructor or other class members. Embarrassing any learner in front of a group may make all learners hesitant to speak. Instructors can ask pointed questions or direct statements toward learners to focus their attention and interest on the subject matter when necessary.

ALLEVIATE FATIGUE

Long lessons are usually fatiguing and reduce the efficiency and effectiveness of teaching and learning. Long lessons should be broken into two or more shorter ones by presenting individual topics separately and by tying the content together with a preview and a summary. Typically, lectures should be no more than 20 minutes. As soon as fatigue is detected, steps should be taken to alleviate the conditions causing the fatigue. Such conditions are particularly dangerous in laboratories, as more accidents occur when individuals are tired or drowsy.

Ventilation and temperature play an important part in the physical comfort of both learners and instructor. A room that is too cold causes discomfort and a room that is too warm is not only uncomfortable, it promotes drowsiness. In rooms where no provision is made for air circulation, instructors should see that windows are open so that sufficient ventilation is possible or that the doors are opened at necessary intervals to allow for air flow. Learners can think more clearly when there is proper ventilation and the temperature is controlled. However, when doors and windows are opened for ventilation, care should be taken to open them no wider than necessary, so that noise and other distractions outside the classroom or laboratory can be avoided.

If boredom or fatigue is suspected, the instructor should check the room temperature and ventilation and then should check to confirm whether the appropriate method is being used to present the material. If the instructor is unable to account for the fatigue of the learners, discussion questions can be directed at learners to get everyone actively involved. If all else fails, learners should be given a short break to stand up and stretch. The enthusiasm and preparation of the instructor is often the best defense against drowsiness and apathy in the classroom.

DEVELOP SEATING ARRANGEMENTS

Traditional forward-facing seating arrangements may not always be the most desirable, especially for group work. A seminar style is appropriate for whole group discussion, whereas cluster seating is appropriate for small group work. No matter what kind of seating arrangement is used, it should be an arrangement that supports the goals and objectives of the lesson or course.

Seating charts, when necessary, can contribute greatly to the effective and efficient management of a classroom. It is not always necessary for the instructor to assign seats. However, a seating chart helps the instructor learn individual names and can aid in maintaining order.

Use Progress Charts

The work of learners should be evaluated, and complete and accurate records should be kept. Progress charts are valuable in keeping up-to-date records. Learners should complete assignments on time. When appropriate, a penalty for late assignments may instill the expectation of personal accountability and responsibility. Learners take greater pride in their work when they know they are being evaluated and when they can see a record of their progress. Progress charts provide a quick overview of each learner's performance. Each progress chart should be confidential, solely used by the instructor and learner.

Commercially prepared progress charts can be purchased. In some cases, instructors may need to develop or customize progress charts for their programs. Whether commercially prepared or instructor-developed, a progress chart should include a list of the important knowledge and skills the learner needs to master, the level of mastery, the date of the mastery check, and the signature or initials of the evaluator. **See Figure 6-1.**

Begin and End Class on Time

Instructors should start and stop classes on time. It is the instructor's responsibility to end class at the scheduled time so that learners can be on time for other classes, jobs, and family obligations. If learners are asking questions that are of interest to only one or a few learners at the end of the class period, the class should be dismissed on time and those who have special questions can remain for the help they need or want.

Maintain a Safe Learning Environment

Technical instructors should be familiar with federal occupational safety and health legislation, which requires safe and healthy working conditions and environments. Instructors should know, practice, and teach the safety and health regulations that relate to their specific area of instruction. Safety and health practices should be integrated throughout the training program, and the learners should be actively involved.

For example, instruction on wearing and using appropriate personal protective clothing and equipment should be an integral part of the instructional program. Personal protective equipment (PPE) may save a learner (or worker) from injury or even death. On-the-job training and internships are valuable experiences that enhance a learner's knowledge; however, simulations and mock scenarios in a safe and supervised environment can also be effective techniques for emphasizing the consequences of a worker's actions. Instructors serve as role models and should wear and use the safety gear that is required for learners.

SAMPLE PROGRESS CHART

CAD/CAM Technician Competency Profile

Directions: Check the appropriate number on the rating scale below to indicate the learner's degree of competency.

Participant Name: _____   Evaluator: _____

Ratings:

NA = Not Applicable
1 = Work requires instruction and constant supervision
2 = Works best with some supervision
3 = Works independently with accuracy and speed

	NA	1	2	3
Reads blueprints	___	___	___	___
Estimates jobs	___	___	___	___
Develops project schedules	___	___	___	___
Creates prints to ANSI standards	___	___	___	___
Programs CNC machine	___	___	___	___

Participant Signature: _____   Date: _____

Evaluator Signature: _____   Date: _____

Figure 6-1. Progress charts provide a quick overview of learner performance.

Instructors should check the physical area in and around the classroom and laboratory to ensure that no safety hazards exist. Stairways, aisles, and floors should be clean and free of debris. Laboratory floors and walkways should be properly marked. The classroom, laboratory, toolroom, and storage space should be clean and organized. In addition, PPE that is in good working condition should be available for each learner. A PPE safety checklist is useful to accomplish this task and avoid oversights. The instructor should also make daily checks of guards, shields, and other PPE to ensure that all are in proper working condition.

Safety instructions for equipment operation and the use of special tools should be posted near each piece of equipment, along with emergency shutdown procedures. An equipment safety checklist helps instructors and learners remain mindful of potential hazards. Every instructor should have a plan for emergencies, and learners should understand the plan and how to carry it out. Horseplay and other disturbances inside the classroom or laboratory that create safety hazards should not be tolerated.

PRACTICE TOOL AND EQUIPMENT SAFETY

The instructor is responsible for the safe working order and operation of all tools and equipment in the classroom and laboratory. Worn-out tools and malfunctioning equipment can lead to accidents and potential lawsuits. Machines must have proper guards and switches. Safety aids such as an eyewash station, shower, master switches, and fire extinguishers should be available where appropriate. PPE such as gloves and safety glasses or goggles should be available to anyone entering a laboratory.

Instructors are responsible for providing instruction to all learners on the safe use of tools and equipment and of PPE. Reasonable accommodations may include assigning note takers or readers to assist learners, providing written communication in alternative formats (large print, audio files/audiotapes, etc.), offering modified examination formats such as oral tests, allowing extended time on tests, permitting the use of certain equipment to aid a learner, providing wheelchair accessibility, and providing preferential seating. Some instructors may choose to have learners create a lab handbook to reinforce the importance of safety.

USE INVENTORY SYSTEMS

Instructors are responsible for the inventory and maintenance of supplies, tools, and equipment in their classroom and laboratory. A spreadsheet or systematic written plan should be developed to facilitate equipment maintenance. An efficient inventory system can also be easily maintained using a software program for inventory control. The system would contain information relating to each tool or piece of equipment such as the date of purchase, the date of service, equipment specifications, or the quantity of consumable material ordered. Maintaining an inventory system is an important task and an excellent assignment for learners.

Summary

One of the first responsibilities of the instructor is to establish an environment where learners feel at ease and know the rules, procedures, and expectations. Creating a safe and positive learning environment promotes effective teaching and learning.

Instructors usually have some control over the physical facilities in terms of the environment. Ensuring that the room is not too warm or too cold and that the environment is comfortable helps learners focus on instruction. Long lessons should be broken into two or more shorter lessons, and lectures should be no more than 20 minutes. If a seating arrangement is used, it should be in conjunction with the goals of the course, for example, cluster seating works well for small group work.

The instructor should use progress charts to track learner assignments. Progress charts can provide a quick overview of an individual learner's work. Securing or developing a systematic way to record learner progress will help in documenting learner competencies and instructional needs.

Attending to safety hazards and plans for responding to emergencies are critical to maintaining a safe instructional program. The instructor may be responsible for the placement and storage of tools. Developing an inventory system for supplies, tools, and equipment will save the instructor time.

Self-Assessment Checklist

HINTS FOR THE HIGHLY EFFECTIVE INSTRUCTOR

Learning Environment Organization

Yes	No	Needs Attention	
☐	☐	☐	1. Is your classroom or laboratory well-lighted, properly heated, and well-ventilated?
☐	☐	☐	2. Are the rules and procedures posted in your classroom and laboratory?
☐	☐	☐	3. Is safety an integral part of your program?
☐	☐	☐	4. Are emergency procedures and safety signs posted in your laboratory?
☐	☐	☐	5. Is your laboratory equipped with first aid equipment such as a first aid kit, an eyewash station, shower, and fire extinguisher?
☐	☐	☐	6. Do you wear appropriate PPE?
☐	☐	☐	7. Do your learners wear appropriate PPE?
☐	☐	☐	8. Do you know how to administer first aid treatment?
☐	☐	☐	9. Do you follow the laws on the labeling, storage, and disposal of hazardous waste?
☐	☐	☐	10. Do you maintain a professional atmosphere in your classroom and laboratory?
☐	☐	☐	11. Do you assign maintenance responsibilities to learners?
☐	☐	☐	12. Is your classroom orderly and neat?
☐	☐	☐	13. Do you maintain an up-to-date inventory of tools and equipment?
☐	☐	☐	14. Do you keep up-to-date maintenance records of equipment?
☐	☐	☐	15. Are the tools and equipment in your laboratory in safe working order?
☐	☐	☐	16. Do you begin and end class on time?
☐	☐	☐	17. Do learners know what is expected of them in terms of classroom and laboratory rules and procedures?
☐	☐	☐	18. Do learners know what is expected of them in terms of work?

ACCOMMODATING SPECIAL POPULATIONS

7

HINTS FOR THE HIGHLY EFFECTIVE INSTRUCTOR

An increasing number of individuals with disabilities are joining the workforce. More than ever before, the implications of accomodating special populations, especially individuals who are eligible for services under the Americans with Disabilities Act, must be recognized and understood.

IDENTIFY NEEDS OF LEARNERS

It is important for instructors to identify learners from special populations before they are admitted into the instructional program. Identification can be made by instructor review of learner records, employers, or by the learners themselves. Instructors need to know the academic ability, technical aptitudes and interests, physical capabilities, and life skills of all learners. This information will give the instructor a better basis for planning and serving all learners, especially those from special populations so that appropriate modifications and accommodations can be made. In addition, the learning environment can be modified to properly address learner needs, such as adjusting the room lighting, providing sound amplification, and/ or changing the size of type displayed.

BE KNOWLEDGEABLE ABOUT EDUCATION LEGISLATION

As educators respond to the changing needs of learners and employers, the instructional environment, and the workplace, it is imperative that they be knowledgeable about legislation that impacts education. Laws have a direct impact on the instructional environment and the workplace. Instructors who understand legislative mandates not only protect themselves and their organization, they also are in a better position to serve all learners effectively and efficiently.

REVIEW SECTION 504 OF THE REHABILITATION ACT OF 1973

Section 504 of the Rehabilitation Act of 1973 prohibits discrimination of otherwise qualified individuals with a disability. The law states that these individuals cannot be excluded from participation in or be denied the benefits of any program or activity receiving federal financial assistance based solely on their disability.

The law was designed to protect individuals with disabilities in an instructional setting or work environment. Until the original passage of the Americans with Disabilities Act in 1990, this section of the law was applied when individuals had claims of discrimination in the workplace.

Review the Individuals with Disabilities Education Act

The Individuals with Disabilities Education Act (IDEA), which became law in 1990, was reauthorized in 2004. This landmark legislation was enacted to ensure a "free and appropriate public education" in the least restrictive environment. Free and appropriate public education means special education and related services that include specially designed instruction that meets the unique needs of an individual covered under the law.

The IDEA requires that an individualized education program (IEP) be developed to meet the unique needs of each individual receiving services. Instructors who participate in the IEP process help other professional personnel and the learner to better understand the safety precautions, subject matter, skills, and dispositions required for successful completion of the instructional program. Instructors of technical subjects should either prepare a checklist or obtain one that lists the skills required to be successful in their program. Also, a list of career paths showing various jobs for which the learner may be prepared will be useful during the planning session. Instructors can help the IEP team set realistic career goals for a learner with special needs.

Implementing an IEP requires administrative skills, such as maintaining the necessary records showing the services provided, critical dates, assessment procedures used, and learner progress. Such records should be kept confidential and in a secure location where they are easily accessible to the instructor.

Review the Americans with Disabilities Act

The Americans with Disabilities Act (ADA) protects individuals with disabilities in educational and work environments. The ADA states that qualified individuals with a disability cannot be discriminated against in the job application process, hiring, advancement, discharge from employment, employee compensation, job training, and other conditions and privileges of employment.

Inherent in the ADA is the requirement that educators and employers provide reasonable modifications or accommodations for any qualified individual with a disability as defined under the law. The ADA generally defines a disability as a physical or mental impairment that substantially limits one or more of a person's major life activities, such as seeing, hearing, walking, standing, sitting, or learning. Any individual with a disability must have the disability documented by appropriate professional personnel. For example, an individual who suffers from a heart condition must have the condition documented by appropriate medical personnel in order to receive special accommodations under the ADA.

Modifications and accommodations should be made on an individual basis to address the specific needs of the individual. Reasonable accommodations may include assigning note takers or readers to assist learners; providing written communication in alternative formats such as in large print, on large displays, or as audio files; offering modified examination formats such as oral tests rather than written tests; allowing extended time on tests; permitting the use of certain equipment to aid a learner or worker; providing wheelchair accessibility; and giving preferential seating.

It is important that educators and employers understand their obligations under the law so that they may provide practical solutions to individual needs for modifications or accommodations.

REVIEW THE EVERY STUDENT SUCCEEDS ACT

The Every Student Succeeds Act (ESSA) was signed into law in 2015. This law reauthorizes the Elementary and Secondary Education Act of 1965 and replaces the No Child Left Behind (NCLB) Act of 2002. The law redefines the federal role in elementary and secondary education and gives states and school districts authority along with accountability.

The ESSA includes provisions that will help ensure success for learners and schools. Below are a few highlights of the law:

- Requires that all students be taught to high academic standards that will prepare them to succeed in college and careers
- Ensures that vital information is provided to educators, families, students, and communities through annual statewide assessments that measure students' progress
- Maintains an expectation that there will be accountability and action to effect positive change in low-performing schools where groups of students are not making progress and where graduation rates are low over extended periods of time
- Upholds critical protections for disadvantaged students
- Expands investments in increasing access to quality preschool education

IDENTIFY APPROPRIATE INSTRUCTIONAL STRATEGIES

Various teaching styles and instructional strategies are necessary to accommodate each learner's knowledge and ability level, needs, interests, and motivation. The instructor should discuss appropriate learning activities and teaching methods, curricular and facilities modifications, scheduling adjustments, class management procedures, and assessment procedures with each learner needing special accommodations and with the IEP team, if appropriate. The learner may be enrolled in the technical education program for a substantial part of the day; thus, such information will alleviate frustration for both the instructor and the learner and save preparation time.

In addition to using instructional strategies based on the needs and abilities of the learners, the requirements of the job should be analyzed. Prior to placing a learner in an instructional environment, the instructor should know the essential tasks that must be performed on the job and the level of performance that is acceptable. For example, if the essential functions of a job require long periods of standing, sitting, walking, lifting, or other kinds of physical activities, appropriate instructional strategies should be used to include the kinds of physical skills required in the workplace. The physical conditions of the work environment should also be considered.

If employees are expected to work in teams, totally alone, or under difficult physical conditions (extreme heat, cold, noise), instructional strategies should take these conditions into account. In addition, the general skills needed for the job, such as ability to read, write, compute, use certain software, solve problems, or make decisions, should be identified, and instructional strategies should be used that require learners to demonstrate these skills.

COLLABORATE WITH OTHERS

Instructors of technical subjects should plan, in collaboration with special education personnel, to provide the best learning environment and activities for all learners. For example, the instructor can recommend and help select appropriate printed materials for a learner with a hearing impairment or audio files for a learner with a visual impairment, or the instructor can provide the special education teacher with a list of terms and concepts used in a particular subject area.

SUMMARY

Whether learners are in a secondary, postsecondary, or industry-based instructional program, individuals with disabilities are protected under the law. Key legislative mandates impact both public and private instructional programs. Section 504 of the Rehabilitation Act of 1973 states that an otherwise qualified individual cannot be excluded from participation in or be denied the benefits of any program or activity receiving federal financial assistance based solely on the disability. The Individuals with Disabilities Education Act ensures a free and appropriate public education in the least restrictive environment. The ADA protects qualified individuals with a disability so that they cannot be discriminated against in educational and employment settings.

Instructors need an objective basis for providing modifications and accommodations and evaluating learner progress. A sound understanding of the provisions of the laws that address instructor responsibility will help to ensure that special groups are served appropriately, adequately, and effectively.

A careful analysis of job tasks will help instructors and employers alike focus on the job to be done rather than the abilities of the individual. Consequently, all individuals in the instructional setting or work environment should be able to realize their potential and contribute to the efficiency and effectiveness of the organization.

Self-Assessment Checklist

HINTS FOR THE HIGHLY EFFECTIVE INSTRUCTOR

ACCOMMODATING SPECIAL POPULATIONS

Yes	No	Needs Attention	
☐	☐	☐	1. Do you accommodate differences in learner abilities?
☐	☐	☐	2. Do you seek out learner records when they are not provided?
☐	☐	☐	3. Do you maintain confidentiality of learner records?
☐	☐	☐	4. Do you keep up-to-date on legislative changes that affect instruction?
☐	☐	☐	5. Do you use different instructional strategies to accommodate various learning styles?
☐	☐	☐	6. Do you participate in the individualized education program (IEP) process?
☐	☐	☐	7. Have you prepared a checklist showing the requirements for success in your program to the IEP team members?
☐	☐	☐	8. Do you follow the goals, objectives, and assessment of the IEP for each learner?
☐	☐	☐	9. Do you modify the instructional environment to accommodate different learner abilities?
☐	☐	☐	10. Do you prepare instruction that prepares learners from special populations for the workplace?
☐	☐	☐	11. Do you collaborate with special education personnel?
☐	☐	☐	12. Do you confer with learners, parents, counselors, teachers, and other appropriate individuals concerning learner progress?

INSTRUCTIONAL ASSESSMENTS

8

Assessment is an integral part of instruction. Without formal feedback from learners, an instructor can only guess at whether the instruction was successful. Accountability for learner achievement is a growing expectation in educational settings, as well as in industry-based training programs. The rise in accountability provides strong encouragement for instructors to connect learner achievement to instructional practices in order to help learners become competent workers.

REVIEW CONTENT

Periodic review of the content covered in each instructional session helps the instructor determine whether learners comprehend the material. Reviews are also of value to learners if the review requires learners to react to problems by thinking through solutions and applying concepts. Review questions should be stated so that learners are required to apply the information when completing activities, homework assignments, and laboratory exercises.

The nature of the subject matter should dictate the frequency and content of the review. For example, it is a waste of time to drill learners on technical information contained in handbooks and manuals that are used as reference guides. These resources can be made available to the learners. In such situations, it is more appropriate to review procedures for locating the reference information, and knowing when and how to use the information, than it is to review the material itself. It is always appropriate to conduct a review at the end of each lesson to provide the preparation step for the next lesson.

UNDERSTAND THE PURPOSE OF ASSESSMENTS

Assessment is the systematic process of collecting quantitative and qualitative data related to learner achievement. Assessment serves two different yet complementary functions. One aim of assessment is to improve learner performance throughout the instructional process. This is formative assessment. Formative assessment should be used throughout the instructional process to make decisions about the design, development, and delivery of instructional courses and programs. Incorrect learner responses provide evidence of content areas where learners need more assistance.

Summative assessment is an assessment given at the conclusion of a course or program to determine the effectiveness of the teaching and learning. In summative assessment, the instructor assesses learner attainment of the knowledge and skills to verify the efficiency and effectiveness of a course or instructional program.

DEVELOP ASSESSMENTS BASED ON PERFORMANCE OBJECTIVES

The primary question instructors should ask is, "Do my assessments address the objectives of the lesson or course?" Performance objectives must be communicated to learners so that learners will know what is expected of them, under what conditions, and to what extent of proficiency. If no objectives have been stated, it is impossible to prepare valid assessments.

Assessments should always align with instructional objectives. **See Figure 8-1.** When alignment does not occur, such as using a multiple-choice assessment to measure the demonstration of a skill, learning is not measured and learners are less motivated to learn.

The first step in developing quality assessment items is to identify the knowledge and skills to be learned and the levels at which learners are expected to perform. These items are called performance objectives. For example, a unit on electrical circuits requires learners to understand electrical safety as well as the operation, diagramming, and troubleshooting of electrical circuits. The assessment will be formed based on the following:

- amount of content to be assessed
- depth of the content to be assessed
- complexity of the knowledge and skills to be assessed
- amount of time allotted for learners to complete the assessment

The format of the assessment and the emphasis given to each topic should be based on the amount of instructional time spent on each topic. For example, if considerably more instructional time was spent on diagramming electrical circuits, learners will expect the assessment to cover diagramming electrical circuits in greater depth than other topics.

A table of assessment specifications serves as a useful framework from which relevant and meaningful items can be developed. **See Figure 8-2.** The instructor lists the skills and knowledge to be acquired in the left margin, with the type of test items to be used listed from left to right across the top of the page. The last column on the right margin shows the emphasis to be given to each topic in the assessment.

OBJECTIVE-ALIGNED ASSESSMENTS	
Type of Objective	Examples of Appropriate Assessments
Define Identify Recognize	☐ Fill-in-the-blank questions ☐ Labeling illustrations or product parts ☐ Matching questions ☐ Multiple-choice questions
Classify Compare Explain Interpret	☐ Concept maps ☐ Oral reports ☐ Problem sets ☐ Written reports/papers
Apply Demonstrate Execute Implement	☐ Labs ☐ Performances ☐ Problem sets ☐ Simulations
Analyze Attribute Differentiate Organize	☐ Case studies ☐ Concept maps ☐ Labs ☐ Projects ☐ Written reports/papers
Assess Critique Evaluate	☐ Journals ☐ Problem sets ☐ Product reviews ☐ Research projects
Create Design Plan Produce	☐ Business plans ☐ Designs ☐ Performances ☐ Prototypes

Figure 8-1. Objective-aligned assessments help motivate learners.

After identifying the content areas to be assessed and the amount of emphasis to be placed on each topic, the next step is to develop the assessment. The instructor should avoid using items that are too general. Items that are too general may fail to assess learner achievement of the intended content. In addition, care should be taken to assess one element of content in each item. An assessment item that covers more than one concept or skill will give misleading results about the concept or skill the learner has acquired. Developing quality assessments requires knowledge, skill, and practice.

Sample Assessment Specifications				
Skills/Knowledge	Facts, Terminology, Concepts*	Problem Solving*	Application and Integration*	Total Percent of Emphasis*
Electrical safety	7	5	10	22
Fundamentals of electrical circuits	6	5	5	16
Reading electrical prints	4	5	5	14
Industrial applications of electrical circuits	7	10	5	22
Troubleshooting electrical circuits	6	10	10	26
Total*	30	35	35	100

*in %

Figure 8-2. Assessment specifications can help instructors plan assessment items based on instructional content.

Use Clear and Concise Assessments

The appearance of an assessment communicates to learners the importance of the subject and the seriousness of the assessment. Correct grammar and punctuation should be used. The format of the assessment instrument should be easy to understand, and the reading level should be appropriate for the content and the learners.

Directions should be as brief as possible and clearly stated. The items should be organized around similar content areas. Easier items should be placed early in the assessment and followed by more difficult items. This builds learner success and confidence. Furthermore, the levels of responses should vary to include activities that require learners to collect, process, and apply information, as well as demonstrate mastery of facts and figures. Assessment items of a given type should be grouped together. For example, all multiple-choice questions should be grouped in one section and all true-false items in another section. **See Figure 8-3.**

Create Answer Keys

Answer keys should be created as an assessment is being developed. This early activity can reveal inconsistencies in item wording and problems with anticipated responses, procedures, or calculations. An answer key also alerts the instructor to response patterns due to the organization of items on the assessment. For example, when using multiple choice items, the instructor should make sure the correct response choices are random, rather than set in a pattern. Also, the instructor can write the page numbers of references that give information on that item on the answer key itself.

Answer keys are often available for commercially prepared assessments. Before the assessment is administered, the answer key should be checked for accuracy.

TYPES OF ASSESSMENT ITEMS			
Type	Format	Advantages	Limitations
Completion	True statement in which one or two key words are replaced by blank spaces in which learner writes the correct response	Minimizes guessing; good for recall of specific facts, figures, and formulas	Measures memory rather than understanding; difficult to develop items that call for one true response
Short answer	Statement or question that requires learners to respond in phrases, sentences, or a short paragraph	Easy to develop; measures written communication skills; indicates understanding of content; minimizes guessing	Scoring may be subjective; may encourage memorization; may have more than one correct response
Essay	A statement, question, or scenario that requires an extended response	Encourages synthesis and evaluation; little opportunity for guessing; easy to construct	Can limit amount of content assessed; time consuming for learners to complete and instructor to score
Multiple choice	Statement stem with one correct answer and typically three distractors	Broad coverage of content; easy to complete; easy to score	Time-consuming to construct; difficult to write plausible distractors; does not measure ability to organize or express ideas
Matching	Two sets of related information arranged in two separate columns, with descriptors in the first column that match named or pictured items in the second column	Allows testing of a large amount of content in a minimum amount of space; objective; easy to score	Difficult to construct items at comprehension level; often fails to measure higher levels of learning
True-False	A complete statement that is either true or false	Allows testing of wide range and large amount of information in short period of time; easy to score	Learners have 50/50 chance of guessing correct answer; may measure memory instead of comprehension; needs large number of items for high reliability

Figure 8-3. Assessment item types are selected for measuring specific competencies.

Analyze Quality of Standardized Assessment Items

After a standardized assessment has been administered and scored, the instructor can review each item for its level of difficulty. The level of item difficulty is determined by the percentage of learners who answered the item correctly. For example, if 17 out of 20 learners answered correctly, the difficulty level of the item (17 ÷ 20) is 85%. This represents a fairly easy item. A difficult item may be one for which only 6 of 20 learners answered correctly. The difficulty level (6 ÷ 20) would be 30%. The difficulty index ranges from 0.00% (no one answered the item correctly) to 100% (everyone answered the item correctly). Item difficulty level is appropriate only for those assessments that include objective test categories such as multiple choice, true-false, matching, and completion.

An analysis of each item can also indicate how well a particular item discriminated between the high-scoring and low-scoring learners. The item discrimination index is determined by selecting the 25% to 33% of learners who earned the highest total scores on the assessment instrument and the 25% to 33% of learners who earned the lowest total scores on the instrument. The number of learners in the low scoring group and high scoring group should be the same. The number of learners in the low scoring group who answered the item correctly is subtracted from the number of learners in the high scoring group who answered the same item correctly. This number is then divided by the number in each group (not the total number in both groups combined).

For example, if there is a total of 40 learners, the instructor may select the highest scoring 11 learners and the lowest scoring 11 learners for the analysis. If all 11 learners in the high scoring group answered the item correctly and 3 in the low scoring group answered the same item correctly, the item discrimination index would be 0.73. The calculation for this is as follows: 11 – 3 = 8, and 8 ÷ 11 = 0.73. The 18 learners scoring in the middle range are not included in the calculation.

This high index indicates that the item discriminated quite well in a positive direction. That is, more learners in the high-scoring group got the item correct than learners in the low-scoring group. When more of the low-scoring learners get an item correct than high-scoring learners, a negative discrimination index results. A negative item discrimination index indicates a problem with the item. The problem may be with the wording of the item or the way in which the content was presented. For a total group of 30 or fewer learners, the instructor should use all scores in the analysis by dividing the total group into two groups.

Use Alternative Forms of Assessment

A variety of assessments should be used so that all learners have an opportunity to demonstrate achievement. The form of assessment used will vary with the purpose of the assessment and the kinds of decisions the instructor will make based on assessment outcomes. Alternative forms of assessment emphasize qualitative information related to learner achievement. **See Figure 8-4.**

ALTERNATIVE FORMS OF ASSESSMENT	
Form	Characteristics
Performance	Application of theory, concepts, and procedures used as formative and summative assessments; requires learner demonstration of competency; measures content impossible to assess in other ways; assesses psychomotor skills; may take place in simulated environment
Product	Learner-produced product that demonstrates mastery of content; demonstrates ability to integrate knowledge and skills
Journal	Learner entries generate awareness of learner background, interests, experiences, and concerns and identify prior knowledge of topic; encourages construction of knowledge as a process
Oral	Oral expression of ideas; allows for immediate feedback; assesses speech; assesses different levels of learning; checklists or rubrics may be used to provide a written record of performance
Portfolio	Purposeful collection of learner-produced documents (papers, videos, artwork, prints, plans, etc.); demonstrates learner growth and progress over time; demonstrates learner achievement; encourages active learner participation in assessment process; permits evaluation of both process and end products; may include letters from instructors or supervisors

Figure 8-4. Alternative forms of assessment provide all learners an opportunity to demonstrate achievement.

Most standardized assessments require learners to recall information and are not alone sufficient for determining competency in a given technical area of study. In contrast, performance assessments provide learners the opportunity to demonstrate field-specific knowledge and skills by performing applications in authentic or simulated settings. Performance assessments can motivate learners to improve their knowledge and skill levels by showing them to what extent their performance meets a standard, and what they need to do to enhance their performance. Performance checklists and job sheets are often used to guide learners through procedures used on the job.

A rubric is another effective form of performance assessment. Rubrics list specific criteria and descriptors clearly stating what a desired performance looks like. Each criterion is rated individually and then added together for a total score of the performance. Rubrics can be used to assess learner performance in a lab, simulation, or job-site setting. For example, the instructor may use a rubric to assess a process or procedure, such as the use of a power tool or the assembly of an engine. The instructor may also use a rubric to assess a learner-generated product such as a 3D prototype or a technical report.

To write or select a rubric for a performance, instructors need to focus on the criteria by which learning will be assessed rather than what the instructor intends to teach. The following guidelines are helpful for writing and selecting rubrics.

- Rubric criteria should be observable and measurable, reflect the most important elements of the learning task, be distinct from other criteria, and be phrased in precise language.
- Rubric descriptors should be observable and measurable, written in consistent and parallel language across the performance scale, and be clearly distinguishable across the performance scale by indicating amount, frequency or intensity.
- The number of rating scale points should reflect the purpose of the rubric.

Learners are typically given a rubric at the beginning of instruction. Learners then perform, receive feedback, practice, and perform again before receiving a score or grade using the same rubric. Because rubrics define quality in terms of objective criteria and standards, they clearly communicate performance expectations, provide informative feedback, and help learners improve performance levels.

Maintain Confidentiality

Instructors need to maintain confidentiality of learners' personal information. The instructor should maintain confidentiality of education records, including assessment scores and grades. The Family Educational Rights and Privacy Act (FERPA) generally prohibits the improper disclosure of personally identifiable information derived from education records. The law applies to all educational agencies and institutions that receive federal funding under any program administered by the U.S. Department of Education. In addition to public elementary and secondary schools, both public and private postsecondary schools generally receive federal funding and are therefore subject to FERPA. Parochial and private schools at the elementary and secondary levels generally do not receive such funding and are therefore not subject to FERPA.

Use Instructor Evaluations

Instructor evaluations provide the instructor with feedback so that instructional effectiveness may be improved. Evaluations help the instructor better understand the way in which learners perceive the teaching-learning process.

The instructor should look for response patterns in the evaluations. While individual opinions are important, it is the majority of like responses that offer the greatest suggestions for improvement. The participation of learners in the evaluation may involve both formal and informal techniques. Learners who are assured that their evaluations will remain anonymous will tend to take the evaluation seriously.

Teaching is a complex activity and numerous teaching effectiveness inventories have been developed. Teaching effectiveness instruments should solicit opinions on relevant topics such as the personal and professional attributes of the instructor, instructional procedures, and the classroom environment. Instructors who do not involve learners in the evaluation of their teaching are missing a valuable opportunity to encourage learners to actively participate in the learning process as well as the opportunity to gain insight into the effectiveness of their teaching.

Document Learner Accomplishments

Scores and grades as indicators of performance are not always the best way to document learner accomplishments. Several different forms of documentation can be used to aid an individual's career path. Each form of documentation represents a specific level of learning. The validity of each form is a key factor in determining how it will be recognized by employers. **See Figure 8-5.** Learners can provide documentation in the form of online badges, certificates, certifications, licenses, and college degrees.

- Badges are online representations of the knowledge, skills, and attitudes a learner has acquired. Open badge systems can be used to earn badges on numerous topics at varying levels of difficulty. Because the infrastructure for badges is still evolving, the quality of knowledge and skills a badge represents may be questioned due to some sources being unaccredited.

- Certificates provide documentation of either course completion or a set of competencies that has been attained. A completion certificate confirms that a learner has completed a course or instructional program. A competency certificate lists the entry-level or job-upgrade competencies a learner has demonstrated during an instructional course or training program.

- Certifications are offered by business/industry and trade associations in many occupational areas. Written and/or performance assessments must be passed in order to document mastery of the knowledge and skills required for a particular certification.

- Licenses are obtained by meeting the requirements set by professional licensing boards in a given occupation or industry and allow the license holder to practice that trade or profession. Licenses require renewal or continuing education credits to remain current
- Degrees are granted by educational institutions to learners who complete a formal course of study. A learner may choose to complete an associate's, bachelor's, master's, or doctoral degree.

Documentation of Learner Accomplishments					
Form	Various providers	Certificates	Certifications	Licenses	Degrees
Awarded by...	Various providers	Educational institutions; training organizations	Business/ industry; trade associations	Professional licensing boards	Educational institutions
Resulting from...	Online activity or course	Course of study	Assessment of knowledge and skills	Meeting requirements	Course of study
Indication of...	Activity or course completion	Education in a specific content area	Mastery of knowledge and skills	Permit to practice a specific trade or profession	Coursework completion
Maintained by...	–	–	Application of skills and reassessment	Renewal exam or continuing Education	–
Examples	Khan Academy Meteorite badges; Chicago city badges	ServSafe Food Handler certificate; forklift operator certificate	Certified Welder (CW); Certified Logistics Technician (CLT)	Master Electrician; Registered Nurse (RN)	Associate's; bachelor's; master's; doctoral

Figure 8-5. Valid documentation of learner accomplishments can greatly aid an individual's career path.

Traditional grades can leave the exact skills the learner has achieved open to interpretation. Currently, competency certificates, industry certifications, professional licenses, and college degrees provide the most valid documentation of learner accomplishments and are recognized by employers. Badges indicate interest and activity but may not be valid documentation of knowledge or skill mastery.

SUMMARY

The primary purpose of assessment is to provide information from which the instructor can answer the question, "Did the learners learn?" Ongoing assessments reveal gaps in learning and help identify instructional methods that may help to enhance learner achievement. If assessments are to yield valid and reliable results, learners must be prepared. Large and small group reviews, sample questions and problems, and study guides help prepare learners to meet lesson, course, and program objectives.

Using a table of assessment specifications showing proportion of total instructional time devoted to specific topics helps ensure that content taught is appropriately and adequately represented on assessments. After administration and scoring of assessments that include objective items such as multiple choice and true-false items, the instructor can ascertain the usefulness of each item by calculating the difficulty and discrimination indices.

Each form of assessment has its appropriate uses, advantages, and limitations. The type of assessments selected for any given body of knowledge or skill should vary with the purpose of the assessment (formative or summative), the predetermined course objectives, learner needs for accommodations, and resources such as time, materials, equipment, and facilities. Performance and product assessments are most useful when evaluating the extent to which learners can perform a skill or procedure. Methods of assessment should be varied to provide opportunities for all learners to demonstrate competency.

Observing confidentiality of learner progress and achievement protects the instructor, learners, and the institution or organization. Learners can provide valuable feedback to instructors for course and program improvement through instructor evaluations. The feedback should be taken seriously and to the extent appropriate and feasible, and lesson, course, or program modifications made. When viewed as a dynamic process, assessment is key to improving both teaching and learning.

Different forms of documentation can be used to represent a learner's accomplishments. The validity of each form of documentation determines whether it will be recognized by employers. Competency certificates, industry certifications, professional licenses, and college degrees are currently recognized by employers as the most valid forms of documenting learning.

Self-Assessment Checklist

HINTS FOR THE HIGHLY EFFECTIVE INSTRUCTOR

INSTRUCTIONAL ASSESSMENTS

Yes	No	Needs Attention	
☐	☐	☐	1. Do you periodically review the content covered in each instructional session?
☐	☐	☐	2. Do you use both formative and summative assessments?
☐	☐	☐	3. Are your assessment items based on performance objectives?
☐	☐	☐	4. Do your assessments include a representative sample of the material covered in the lessons?
☐	☐	☐	5. Do the items on your assessments align with the lesson objectives?
☐	☐	☐	6. Do the type and number of assessment items used correspond to the importance of the knowledge and skill needed to succeed in the workplace?
☐	☐	☐	7. Are your assessments clear and concise?
☐	☐	☐	8. Do you create an answer key when an assessment is being developed?
☐	☐	☐	9. Do you use a variety of items on each assessment?
☐	☐	☐	10. Do you analyze the quality of standardized assessment items?
☐	☐	☐	11. Do you use alternative forms of assessment?
☐	☐	☐	12. Do you use rubrics to grade performance assessments?
☐	☐	☐	13. Do you review material before a test?
☐	☐	☐	14. Do you maintain confidentiality of learner information?
☐	☐	☐	15. Do you share progress results with learners?
☐	☐	☐	16. Does your institution issue completion certificates or competency certificates?
☐	☐	☐	17. Do you help learners prepare for certification exams?
☐	☐	☐	18. Do you help learners prepare for licensing exams?
☐	☐	☐	19. Does your institution issue degrees?
☐	☐	☐	20. Do you use instructor evaluations as a means of acquiring learner feedback for improving your program?
☐	☐	☐	21. Do you conduct follow-up studies to gauge the satisfaction of employers who have hired your graduates?

PROFESSIONAL DEVELOPMENT

9

HINTS FOR THE HIGHLY EFFECTIVE INSTRUCTOR

Possessing knowledge of a subject area is not enough for an instructor. Continued development of professional competencies is necessary for effective and efficient instruction. Instructors who fail to keep up with the latest technology, innovations, and trends in their technical fields may find that some learners know more about new developments than they do. Failure to present current information with the latest equipment that represents the industry results in ineffective learning, a loss of learner interest in the subject, and the integrity of the instructor and program being compromised.

TAKE RESPONSIBILITY FOR PROFESSIONAL DEVELOPMENT

There are numerous opportunities for professional development. New legislation, policies, and program guidelines are presented at state-supported professional development activities. Colleges and universities often offer special courses, seminars, and workshops to help update the technical and professional competencies of instructors as well as facilitate the acquisition of new knowledge. Professional and industry associations also provide special conferences, meetings, and resource materials to enhance the professional development of instructors.

INCREASE SUBJECT MATTER KNOWLEDGE

Subject matter knowledge is acquired through experience in the field and formal training. Experience in the field is necessary for establishing instructor credibility. Most instructors have industry experience but may be lacking in a particular area. In addition, as technology advances, the instructor must be proactive in acquiring new knowledge and skills.

Technical update seminars held by recognized companies can present new products, tools, and equipment to instructors. Conferences can offer a wealth of new information from industry professionals and equipment vendors. These environments may also present the opportunity for instructors to share common problems and solutions with peers. Other methods of acquiring information include reading trade publications, attending classes, and participating in professional organizations.

Establish an Advisory Committee

Local business and industry representatives have expertise that can be an excellent resource for an instructional program. An instructor can tap into these resources by establishing an advisory committee. An advisory committee consists of members who possess a variety of skills and backgrounds and can offer support and program direction from an industry perspective. Local business and industry representatives are usually supportive of instructional programs because they provide trained workers to the community. Joining an interest group on LinkedIn® offers continuing communication among industry professionals on a specific area of expertise.

Summary

Instructors must set the example for learners and take responsibility for their own professional development. Instructors can subscribe to professional journals, seek out new resource materials, and network with colleagues to gain information and share ideas. Participating in conferences and seminars is also a way for instructors to increase their technical and instructional knowledge.

Self-Assessment Checklist

PROFESSIONAL DEVELOPMENT

Yes	No	Needs Attention	
☐	☐	☐	1. Do you read professional education literature?
☐	☐	☐	2. Are you a member of one or more professional associations or organizations?
☐	☐	☐	3. Have you chaired a committee or worked actively within a professional association or organization?
☐	☐	☐	4. Do you take courses to enhance your instructional efficiency?
☐	☐	☐	5. Have you given a presentation at a professional meeting?
☐	☐	☐	6. Do you assist with local school functions?
☐	☐	☐	7. Do you visit businesses and industries that may hire graduates of your program?
☐	☐	☐	8. Do you know the supply and demand for employees in your field?
☐	☐	☐	9. Have you written a report or news article about your program?
☐	☐	☐	10. Do you maintain an active advisory committee for your program?

REFERENCES

HINTS FOR THE HIGHLY EFFECTIVE INSTRUCTOR

Brookhart, S. M. (2013). *How to Create and Use Rubrics for Formative Assessment and Grading.* Alexandria, VA: Association for Supervision and Curriculum Development.

Brookhart, S. M. (2014). *How to Design Questions and Tasks to Assess Student Thinking.* Alexandria, VA: Association for Supervision and Curriculum Development.

Emmer, E. T., Evertson, C. M., Clements, B. S., & Worsham, M. E. (1997). *Classroom Management for Secondary Teachers* (4th ed.). Boston: Allyn & Bacon.

Hall, B. H., & Marsh, R. J. (2003). *Legal Issues in Career and Technical Education.* Homewood, IL: American Technical Publishers.

Miller, W. R., & Miller, M. F. (2014). *Essential Teaching Skills: Strategies for the Highly Effective Instructor.* Orland Park, IL: American Technical Publishers.

Miller, W. R., & Miller, M. F. (2009). *Instructors and Their Jobs* (4th ed.). Orland Park, IL: American Technical Publishers.

Pahomov, L. (2014). *Authentic Learning in the Digital Age.* Alexandria, VA: Association for Supervision and Curriculum Development.

Sarkees-Wircenski, M., & Scott, J. (2003). *Special Populations in Career and Technical Education.* Homewood, IL: American Technical Publishers.

Scott, J. (2014). *Overview of Career and Technical Education* (5th ed.). Orland Park, IL: American Technical Publishers.

Storm, G. (1993). *Managing the Occupational Education Laboratory* (2nd ed.). Ann Arbor, MI: Prakken Publications.